Core Data

Florian Kugler, Daniel Eggert

For more books and articles visit us at http://objc.io
Email: mail@objc.io
Twitter: @objcio

Introduction

Part 1
Core Data Basics

1   Hello Core Data

2   Relationships

3   Data Types

Part 2
Understanding Core Data

Part 3
Concurrency and Syncing

8   Working with Multiple Contexts

9   Problems with Multiple Contexts

Part 4
Advanced Topics

10   Predicates

11   Text

Introduction

Core Data is Apple's object graph management and persistency framework for iOS, OS X, watchOS, and tvOS. If your app needs to persist structured data, Core Data is the obvious solution to look into: it's already there, it's actively maintained by Apple, and it has been around for more than 10 years. It's a mature, battle-tested code base.

Nevertheless, Core Data can also be somewhat confusing at first; it's flexible, but it's not obvious how to best use its API. That said, the goal of this book is to help you get off to a flying start. We want to provide you with a set of best practices — ranging from simple to advanced use cases — so that you can take advantage of Core Data's capabilities without getting lost in unnecessary complexities.

For example, Core Data is often blamed for being difficult to use in a multithreaded environment. But Core Data has a very clear and consistent concurrency model. Used correctly, it helps you avoid many of the pitfalls inherent to concurrent programming. The remaining complexities are not specific to Core Data but rather to concurrency itself. We go into those issues in the chapter about problems that can occur with multiple contexts, and in another chapter, we show a practical example of a background syncing solution.

Similarly, Core Data often has the reputation of being slow. If you try to use it like a relational database, you'll find that it has a high performance overhead compared to, for example, using SQLite directly. However, when using Core Data correctly – treating it as an object graph management system – there are actually quite a few places where it ends up being faster due to its built-in caches and object management. Furthermore, the higher-level API lets you focus on optimizing the performance-critical parts of your application instead of reimplementing persistency from scratch. Throughout this book, we'll also describe best practices to keep Core Data performant. We'll take a look at how to approach performance issues in the dedicated chapter about performance, as well as in the profiling chapter.

How This Book Approaches Core Data

This book shows how to use Core Data with working examples — it is not an extended API manual. We deliberately focus on best practices within the context of complete examples. We do so because, in our experience, stringing all the parts of Core Data together correctly is where most challenges occur.

In addition, this book provides an in-depth explanation of Core Data's inner workings. Understanding this flexible framework helps you make the right decisions and, at the same time, keep your code simple and approachable. This is particularly true when it comes to concurrency and performance.

Sample Code

You can get the complete source code for an example app on GitHub[1]. We're using this app in many parts of the book to show problems and solutions in the context of a larger project.

Please note that the sample code will sometimes deviate from the code examples early on in the book. This is because the full source code is for the sample project in its final form, whereas the early chapters describe the project in its earlier, simpler stages.

Structure

In the first part of the book, we will start to build a simple version of our app to demonstrate the basic principles of how Core Data works and how you should use it. Even if the early examples sound trivial to you, we still recommend that you go over these sections of the book, as the later, more complex examples build on top of the best practices and techniques introduced early on. Furthermore, we want to show you that Core Data can be extremely useful for simple use cases as well.

The second part focuses on an in-depth understanding of how all the parts of Core Data play together. We will look in detail at what happens when you access data in various ways, as well as what occurs when you insert or manipulate data. We cover much more than what's necessary to write a simple Core Data application, but this knowledge can come in handy once you're dealing with larger or more complex setups. Building on this foundation, we conclude this part with a chapter about performance considerations.

The third part starts with describing a general purpose syncing architecture to keep your local data up to date with a network service. Then we go into the details of how you can use Core Data with multiple managed object contexts at once. We present different options to set up the Core Data stack and discuss

1 https://github.com/objcio/core-data

their advantages and disadvantages. The last chapter in this part describes how to navigate the additional complexity of working with multiple contexts concurrently.

The fourth part deals with advanced topics like advanced predicates, searching and sorting text, how to migrate your data between different model versions, and tools and techniques to profile the performance of your Core Data stack. It also includes a chapter that introduces the basics of relational databases and the SQL query language from the perspective of Core Data. If you're not familiar with these, it can be helpful to go through this crash course, especially to understand potential performance issues and the profiling techniques required to tackle them.

A Note on Swift

Throughout this book, we use Swift for all examples. We embrace Swift's language features — like generics, protocols, and extensions — to make working with Core Data's API elegant, easier, and safer.

However, all the best practices and patterns we show in Swift can be applied in an Objective-C code base as well. The implementation will be a bit different in some aspects, in order to fit the language, but the underlying principles remain the same.

Conventions for Optionals

Swift provides the Optional data type, which enables and forces us to explicitly think about and handle cases of missing values. We are big fans of this feature, and we use it consistently throughout all examples.

Consequently, we avoid using Swift's ! operator to force-unwrap optionals (along with its usage to define implicitly unwrapped types). We consider this to be a code smell, since it undermines the safety that comes from having an optional type in the first place.

That being said, the single exception to this rule is properties that have to be set but cannot be set at initialization time. Examples of this are Interface Builder outlets or required delegate properties. In these cases, using implicitly unwrapped optionals follows the "crash early" rule: we want to notice immediately when one of these required properties has not been set.

Conventions for Error Handling

There are a few methods in Core Data that can throw errors. Our rationale for how we handle errors is based on the fact that there are different kinds of errors. We will differentiate between errors due to logic failures and all other errors.

Logic errors are the result of the programmer making a mistake. They should be handled by fixing the code and not by trying to recover dynamically.

An example is when code tries to read a file that is part of the app bundle. Since the app bundle is read-only, a file either exists or doesn't, and its content will never change. If we fail to open or parse a file in the app bundle, that's a logic error.

For these kinds of errors, we use Swift's **try**! or fatalError () in order to crash as early as possible.

The same line of thought goes for casting with **as**!: if we know that an object must be of a certain type, and the only reason it could fail would be due to a logic error, we actually want the app to crash.

Quite often we will use Swift's **guard** keyword to be more expressive about what went wrong. For example, when a fetched results controller returns an object of type NSManagedObject and we know that it actually must be a specific subclass, we guard the downcast and exit with a fatal error in case of failure:

```
func objectAtIndexPath(indexPath: NSIndexPath) -> Object {
    guard let result = fetchedResultsController.objectAtIndexPath(indexPath)
        as? Object else
    {
        fatalError("Unexpected object at \(indexPath)")
    }
    return result
}
```

For recoverable errors that are not logic errors, we use Swift's error propagation method: throwing or re-throwing errors.

Part 1
Core Data
Basics

Hello Core Data

In this chapter, we're going to build a simple app that uses Core Data. In the process, we'll explain the basic architecture of Core Data and how to use it correctly for this scenario. Naturally, there's more to say about almost every aspect we touch on in this chapter, but rest assured we will revisit all these topics in more detail later on.

This chapter covers all the Core Data-related aspects of the example app; it's not meant to be a step-by-step tutorial to build the whole app from scratch. We recommend that you look at the full code on GitHub[1] to see all the different parts in context.

The example app consists of one simple screen with a table view and a live camera feed at the bottom. After snapping a picture, we extract an array of dominant colors from it, store this color scheme (we call it a "mood"), and update the table view accordingly:

Figure 1.1: The sample app "Moody"

1 https://github.com/objcio/core-data

Core Data Architecture

Before we start building the example app, we'll first take a look at the major building blocks of Core Data to get a better understanding of its architecture. We will come back to the details of how all the parts play together in part two.

A basic Core Data stack consists of four major parts: the managed objects (NSManagedObject), the managed object context (NSManagedObjectContext), the persistent store coordinator (NSPersistentStoreCoordinator), and the persistent store (NSPersistentStore):

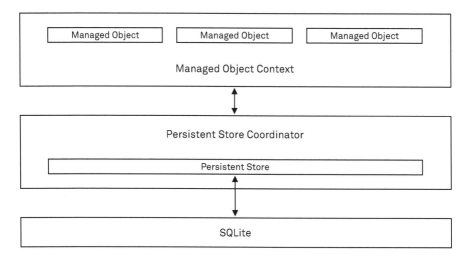

Figure 1.2: The components of a basic Core Data stack

The managed objects at the top of this graph are the most interesting part and will be our model objects — in this case, instances of the Mood class. Mood needs to be a subclass of NSManagedObject — that's how it integrates with the rest of Core Data. Each Mood instance represents one of the *moods*, i.e. snapshots the user takes with the camera.

Our mood objects are *managed* objects. They are managed by Core Data, which means that they live in a specific context: a managed object context. The managed object context keeps track of its managed objects and all the changes you make to them, i.e. insertions, deletions, and updates. And each managed object knows which context it belongs to. Core Data supports multiple contexts, but let's not get ahead of ourselves: for most simple setups, like the one in this chapter, we will only use one context.

The context connects to a persistent store coordinator. It sits between the persistent store and the managed object context and takes a coordinating role between these two. As with the contexts, you can also use a combination of multiple persistent stores and store coordinators. You will rarely need this, though. And for now, we will just use one context, one persistent store coordinator, and one persistent store.

The persistent store coordinator is a rather opaque object that sits right at the center of the stack, and you'll usually never interact with it directly. Nevertheless, it's a very important piece that we will look at in more detail in the chapter about accessing data in part two.

The last piece to the puzzle is the persistent store. It is part of the persistent store coordinator (an NSPersistentStore instance is tied to one particular coordinator), and it takes care of storing and loading the data from the underlying data store. Most of the time, you will use the SQLite flavor of the persistent store, which relies on the widespread SQLite database to store data on disk. Core Data provides options for other store types (XML, binary, in-memory), but we don't need to worry about those at this point.

Data Modeling

Core Data stores structured data. In order to use Core Data, we first have to create a data model (a schema, if you will) that describes the structure of our data.

You can define a data model in code. It's easier, however, to use Xcode's model editor to create and edit an .xcdatamodeld bundle. When you start with an empty Xcode template for an iOS or OS X app, you create a data model by going to File > New and choosing "Data Model" from the Core Data section. If you clicked the "Use Core Data" checkbox when first creating the project, an empty data model has already been created for you.

However, you don't need to click the "Use Core Data" checkbox to use Core Data in your project — on the contrary, we suggest you don't, since we'll throw out all the generated boilerplate code anyway.

Once you select the data model in the project navigator, Xcode's data model editor opens up, and we can start to work on our model.

Entities and Attributes

Entities are the building blocks of the data model. As such, an entity should represent a piece of data that's meaningful to your application. For example, in our case, we create an entity called *Mood*, which has two attributes: one for the colors, and one for the date of the snapshot. By convention, entity names start with an uppercase letter, analogous to class names.

Core Data supports a number of different data types out of the box: numeric types (integers and floating-point values of different sizes, as well as decimal numbers), strings, booleans, dates, and binary data, as well as the transformable type that stores any object conforming to NSCoding or objects for which you provide a custom value transformer.

For the *Mood* entity, we create two attributes: one of type Date (named date), and one of type Transformable (named colors). Attribute names should start with a lowercase letter, just like properties in a class or a struct. The colors attribute holds an array of UIColor objects. Since NSArray and UIColor are already NSCoding compliant, we can store such an array directly in a transformable attribute:

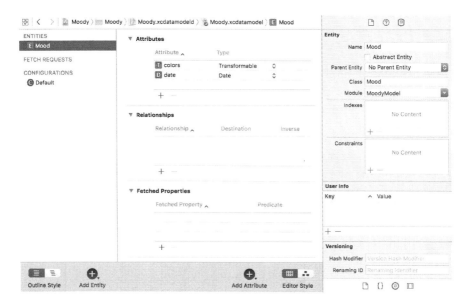

Figure 1.3: The *Mood* entity in Xcode's model editor

Attribute Options

Both attributes have a few more options we need to adjust. We mark the date attribute as non-optional and indexed, and the color sequence attribute as non-optional.

Non-optional attributes have to have a valid value assigned to them in order to be able to save the data. Marking an attribute as indexed creates an index on the underlying SQLite database table. An index speeds up finding and sorting records by this attribute at the cost of reduced performance when inserting new records and some additional storage space. In our case, we will display the mood objects sorted by date, so it makes sense to index this attribute. We go into more depth on the topic of indexes in the chapters about performance and profiling:

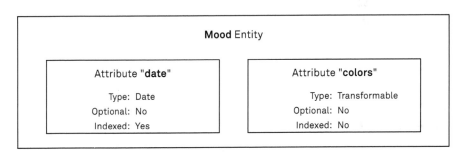

Figure 1.4: The attributes of the *Mood* entity

Managed Object Subclasses

Now that we've created the data model, we have to create a managed object subclass that represents the *Mood* entity. The entity is just a description of the data that belongs to each mood. In order to work with this data in our code, we need a class that has the properties corresponding to the attributes we defined on the entity.

It's good practice to name those classes by what they represent, without adding suffixes like Entity to them. Our class will simply be called Mood and not MoodEntity. Both the entity and the class will be called Mood, and that's perfectly fine.

For creating the class, we advise against using Xcode's code generation tool (Editor > Create NSManagedObject Subclass...) and instead suggest simply writing it by hand. In the end, it's just a few lines of code you have to type once, and there is the upside of being fully in control of how you write it. Additionally, it makes the process more transparent — you'll see that there is no magic involved.

Our *Mood* entity looks like this in code:

```
public final class Mood: ManagedObject {
    @NSManaged public private(set) var date: NSDate
    @NSManaged public private(set) var colors: [UIColor]
}
```

The superclass, ManagedObject, is simply an empty subclass of NSManagedObject:

```
public class ManagedObject: NSManagedObject {
}
```

We only need the ManagedObject superclass because of the way generic type constraints work in Swift. We'll mention this again when it becomes relevant, but for now you can just consider it to be equivalent to NSManagedObject.

The **@NSManaged** attributes on the properties in the Mood class tell the compiler that those properties are backed by Core Data attributes. Core Data implements them in a very different way, but we'll talk about this in more detail in part two. The **private(set)** access control modifiers specify that both properties are publicly readable, but not writable. Core Data does not enforce such a read-only policy, but with those annotations in our class definition, the compiler will.

In our case, there's no need to expose the aforementioned attributes to the world as writable. We will create a helper method later on to insert new moods with specific values upon creation, and we never want to change these values after that. In general, it's best to only publicly expose those properties and methods of your model objects that you really need to expose.

To make Core Data aware of our Mood class, and to associate it with the *Mood* entity, we select the entity in the model editor and type the class name in the data model inspector. Since we're using Swift modules, we also have to select the module the class is defined in.

Setting Up the Stack

Now that we have the first version of our data model and the Mood class in place, we can set up a basic Core Data stack. We expose the following function to create the main managed object context. We will then use this context throughout the app:

```
private let StoreURL = NSURL.documentsURL
    .URLByAppendingPathComponent("Moody.moody")

public func createMoodyMainContext() -> NSManagedObjectContext {
    let bundles = [NSBundle(forClass: Mood.self)]
    guard let model = NSManagedObjectModel
        .mergedModelFromBundles(bundles)
        else { fatalError("model not found") }
    let psc = NSPersistentStoreCoordinator(managedObjectModel: model)
    try! psc.addPersistentStoreWithType(NSSQLiteStoreType, configuration: nil,
        URL: StoreURL, options: nil)
    let context = NSManagedObjectContext(
        concurrencyType: .MainQueueConcurrencyType)
    context.persistentStoreCoordinator = psc
    return context
}
```

Let's go through this step by step.

First, we get the bundle where our managed object model resides. We use NSBundle(forClass:) for this so that the code still works if we move it to another module. Then we load the data model using NSManagedObjectModel's helper method, mergedModelFromBundles(_:). This method looks for all models in the specified bundles and merges them into one managed object model. Since we only have one model, it will simply load that one.

Next, we create the persistent store coordinator. After initializing it with the object model, we add a persistent store of type NSSQLiteStoreType to it. The URL where the store should reside is defined in the private StoreURL constant and points to *Moody.moody* in the documents directory. If the database already exists in this location, it will be opened; otherwise, Core Data will create a new one.

The addPersistentStoreWithType(_:configuration:URL:options:) method potentially throws an error, so we have to either handle it explicitly, or call it using the **try**! keyword, which will result in a runtime error (if an error occurs).

In our case, we use **try**!, since there is no feasible way to recover from such an error anyway.

Lastly, we create the managed object context by initializing it with the .MainQueueConcurrencyType option and assigning the coordinator to the context's persistentStoreCoordinator property. The .MainQueueConcurrencyType specifies that this context is tied to the main thread where all our user interface work is being done. We can safely access this context and its managed objects from anywhere in our UI code. We'll say more about this when we look at using Core Data with multiple contexts.

Since we have encapsulated all this boilerplate code in a neat helper function, we can initialize the main context from the application delegate with a single call to createMoodyMainContext():

```
class AppDelegate: UIResponder, UIApplicationDelegate {
    let managedObjectContext = createMoodyMainContext()
    // ...
}
```

Showing the Data

Now that we have initialized the Core Data stack, we can use the managed object context we created in the application delegate to query for data that we want to display.

In order to use the managed object context in the view controllers of our app, we hand the context object from the application delegate to the first view controller, and later, from there to other view controllers in the hierarchy. We make this structure more explicit by defining a protocol:

```
protocol ManagedObjectContextSettable: class {
    var managedObjectContext: NSManagedObjectContext! { get set }
}
```

Now we make the first view controller in the hierarchy conform to this protocol:

```
class RootViewController: UIViewController, ManagedObjectContextSettable {
    var managedObjectContext: NSManagedObjectContext!
    // ...
}
```

Finally, we can set the context on the root view controller in the application delegate, which conforms to the new protocol:

```
func application(application: UIApplication,
    didFinishLaunchingWithOptions launchOptions: [NSObject: AnyObject]?)
    -> Bool
{
    // ...
    guard let vc = window?.rootViewController
        as? ManagedObjectContextSettable
        else { fatalError("Wrong view controller type") }
    vc.managedObjectContext = managedObjectContext
    // ...
}
```

In the same fashion, we hand over the managed object context from the root view controller to the table view controller that actually needs the context to display the data. Since our sample project uses a Storyboard, we hook into the view controller's prepareForSegue(_:sender:) method to accomplish this:

```
override func prepareForSegue(segue: UIStoryboardSegue,
    sender: AnyObject?)
{
    switch segueIdentifierForSegue(segue) {
    case .EmbedNavigation:
        guard let nc = segue.destinationViewController
                as? UINavigationController,
            let vc = nc.viewControllers.first
                as? ManagedObjectContextSettable
            else { fatalError("wrong view controller type") }
        vc.managedObjectContext = managedObjectContext
    }
}
```

The pattern is very similar to what we did in the application delegate, but now we first have to go through the navigation controller to get to the MoodsTableViewController instance, which conforms to the ManagedObjectContextSettable protocol.

In case you were wondering where the segueIdentifierForSegue(_:) comes from, we took this pattern from the session Swift in Practice, presented at WWDC 2015. It's a nice use case of protocol extensions in Swift used to make segues more explicit and to let the compiler check if we've handled all cases.

To display the mood objects — we don't have any yet, but we will take care of that in a bit — we use a table view in combination with Core Data's NSFetchedResultsController. This controller class watches out for changes in our dataset and informs us about those changes in a way that makes it very easy to update the table view accordingly.

Fetch Requests

As the name indicates, a fetch request describes what data is to be fetched from the persistent store and how. We will use it to retrieve all Mood instances, sorted by their creation dates. Fetch requests also allow very complex filtering in order to only retrieve specific objects. In fact, fetch requests are so complex that we'll save most of the details for later.

One important thing we want to point out now is this: every time you execute a fetch request, Core Data goes through the complete Core Data stack, all the way to the file system. By contract, a fetch request is a round trip: from the context, through the persistent store coordinator and the persistent store, down to SQLite, and then all the way back.

While fetch requests are very powerful workhorses, they incur a lot of work. Executing a fetch request is a comparatively expensive operation. We will go into more detail in part two about why this is and how to avoid these costs. For now, we just want you to remember that you should use fetch requests thoughtfully, and that they are a point of potential performance bottlenecks. Often, they can be avoided by traversing relationships, which we'll also cover later.

Let's turn back to our example. Here's how we could create a fetch request to retrieve all Mood instances from Core Data, sorted by their creation dates in a descending order (we will clean this code up shortly):

```
let request = NSFetchRequest(entityName: "Mood")
let sortDescriptor = NSSortDescriptor(key: "date", ascending: false)
request.sortDescriptors = [sortDescriptor]
request.fetchBatchSize = 20
```

The entityName is the name our *Mood* entity has in the data model. The fetchBatchSize property tells Core Data to only fetch a certain number of mood objects at a time. There's a lot of magic going on behind the scenes for this to work; we will dive into the mechanics of it all in the chapter about accessing data. We're using 20 as batch size, because that roughly corresponds to twice the number of items on screen at the same time. We'll come back to adjusting the batch size in the performance chapter.

Simplified Model Classes

Before we go ahead and use this fetch request, we will take a step back and add a few things to our model class to keep our code easy to use and maintain.

We want to demonstrate a way to create fetch requests that better separates concerns. This pattern will also come in handy later for many other aspects of the example app as we expand it.

Protocols play a central role in Swift. We'll add a protocol that our Mood model class will implement. In fact, all model classes we add later will implement this too — and so should yours:

```swift
public protocol ManagedObjectType: class {
    static var entityName: String { get }
    static var defaultSortDescriptors: [NSSortDescriptor] { get }
}
```

We will make use of Swift's protocol extensions to add a default implementation for this protocol, returning an empty array for defaultSortDescriptors. Additionally, we'll add a computed property to get a fetch request with the default sort descriptors for this entity:

```swift
extension ManagedObjectType {
    public static var defaultSortDescriptors: [NSSortDescriptor] {
        return []
    }

    public static var sortedFetchRequest: NSFetchRequest {
        let request = NSFetchRequest(entityName: entityName)
        request.sortDescriptors = defaultSortDescriptors
        return request
    }
}
```

Now we add conformance for this protocol to the Mood class. We implement the static entityName property and add custom default sort descriptors. We want the Mood instances to be sorted by date by default (just like the fetch request we created before):

```
extension Mood: ManagedObjectType {
    public static var entityName: String {
        return "Mood"
    }

    public static var defaultSortDescriptors: [NSSortDescriptor] {
        return [NSSortDescriptor(key: "date", ascending: false)]
    }
}
```

With this extension, we can create the same fetch request as above, like this:

```
let request = Mood.sortedFetchRequest
request.fetchBatchSize = 20
```

We will later build upon this pattern and add more convenience methods to the ManagedObjectType protocol — for example, when creating fetch requests with specific predicates or finding objects of this type. You can check out all the extensions on ManagedObjectType in the sample code[2].

Using the ManagedObjectType protocol, we've now encapsulated the entity's name in an extension of the model class itself, and we've added a convenient way to get a preconfigured fetch request for the Mood class.

At this point, it might seem like an unnecessary overhead for what we've gained. It's a much cleaner design, though, and a better foundation to build upon. As our app grows, we will make more use of this pattern. We don't have to hardcode this information in the places where we use it. We have improved the separation of concerns. With these changes, the Mood class *knows* what its entity is, and what its default sort order is.

Fetched Results Controller

We use the NSFetchedResultsController class to mediate between the model and view. In our case, we use it to keep the table view up to date with the mood objects in Core Data, but fetched results controllers can also be used in other scenarios — for example, with a collection view.

The main advantage of using a fetched results controller — instead of simply executing a fetch request ourselves and handing the results to the table view —

2 https://github.com/objcio/core-data/blob/master/SharedCode/ManagedObject.swift

is that it informs us about changes in the underlying data in a way that makes it easy to update the table view. To achieve this, the fetched results controller listens to a notification, which gets posted by the managed object context whenever the data in the context changes (more on this in the chapter about changing and saving data). Respecting the sorting of the underlying fetch request, it figures out which objects have changed their positions, which have been newly inserted, etc., and reports those changes to its delegate:

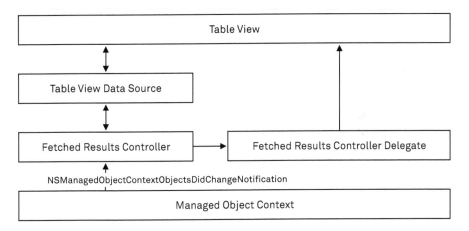

Figure 1.5: How the fetched results controller interacts with the table view

To initialize the fetched results controller for the mood table view, we call setupTableView() from viewDidLoad() in the UITableViewController subclass. setupTableView() uses the fetch request above to create a fetched results controller and, in turn, pass that to a custom class that wraps all the boilerplate delegate code of the fetched results controller:

```
private func setupTableView() {
    // ...
    let request = Mood.sortedFetchRequest
    request.returnsObjectsAsFaults = false
    request.fetchBatchSize = 20
    let frc = NSFetchedResultsController(fetchRequest: request,
        managedObjectContext: managedObjectContext,
        sectionNameKeyPath: nil, cacheName: nil)
    let dataProvider = FetchedResultsDataProvider(
        fetchedResultsController: frc, delegate: self)
    // ...
}
```

The FetchedResultsDataProvider implements the following three delegate methods of the fetched results controller, which inform us about changes in the underlying data:

1. controllerWillChangeContent(_:)

2. controller(_:didChangeObject:...)

3. controllerDidChangeContent(_:)

We could simply implement the above methods in the view controller class. However, this would clutter up the view controller with boilerplate code, which we'll need any time we want to use a fetched results controller. Therefore, we're going to do this right from the start and encapsulate the delegate methods in the reusable FetchedResultsDataProvider class:

```
class FetchedResultsDataProvider<Delegate: DataProviderDelegate>: NSObject,
    NSFetchedResultsControllerDelegate, DataProvider
{
    // ...
    init (fetchedResultsController: NSFetchedResultsController,
        delegate: Delegate)
    {
        self.fetchedResultsController = fetchedResultsController
        self.delegate = delegate
        super.init ()
        fetchedResultsController.delegate = self
        try! fetchedResultsController.performFetch()
    }

    func controllerWillChangeContent(controller: NSFetchedResultsController) {
        // ...
    }

    func controller(controller:  NSFetchedResultsController,
        didChangeObject anObject: AnyObject,
        atIndexPath indexPath: NSIndexPath?,
        forChangeType type: NSFetchedResultsChangeType,
        newIndexPath: NSIndexPath?)
    {
        // ...
    }

    func controllerDidChangeContent(controller: NSFetchedResultsController) {
        delegate.dataProviderDidUpdate(updates)
```

```
    }
}
```

During initialization, the FetchedResultsDataProvider sets itself as the fetched results controller's delegate. Then it calls performFetch(_:) to load the data from the persistent store. Since this call can throw an error, we prefix it with **try**! to crash early, since this would indicate a programming error.

In the delegate methods, the data provider class gathers all the changes reported from the fetched results controller in an array of DataProviderUpdate enum instances:

```
enum DataProviderUpdate<Object> {
    case Insert(NSIndexPath)
    case Update(NSIndexPath, Object)
    case Move(NSIndexPath, NSIndexPath)
    case Delete(NSIndexPath)
}
```

At the end of an update cycle (in controllerDidChangeContent(_:)), the data provider hands the updates over to its delegate.

We can reuse this class later on for other table views or even for collection views. Please check the sample project for the full source code[3] of this class.

With the fetched results controller and its delegate in place, we can now move on to actually showing the data in the table view. For this, we have to implement the table view's data source methods. We'll follow a similar pattern as with the fetched results controller's delegate methods and encapsulate the data source in a separate reusable class. Here's how our classes wrapping the fetched results controller delegate and table view data source play together with the other parts:

---

3 https://github.com/objcio/core-data/blob/master/Moody/Moody/FetchedResultsDataProvider.swift

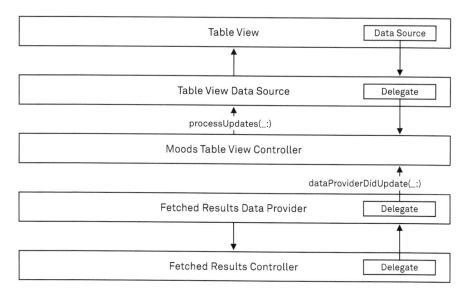

Figure 1.6: The data provider and data source classes encapsulate the boilerplate code to keep a table view up to date with a fetched results controller

As with the data provider, we initialize the data source instance in setupTableView(), passing in the previously created data provider:

```
private func setupTableView() {
    // ...
    dataSource = TableViewDataSource(tableView: tableView,
        dataProvider: dataProvider, delegate: self)
}
```

The data source object can now use the data provider to get the information it needs to implement the table view's data source methods:

```
func tableView(tableView: UITableView, numberOfRowsInSection section: Int)
    -> Int
{
    return dataProvider.numberOfItemsInSection(section)
}

func tableView(tableView: UITableView,
    cellForRowAtIndexPath indexPath: NSIndexPath) -> UITableViewCell
{
    let  object = dataProvider.objectAtIndexPath(indexPath)
    let  identifier  = delegate.cellIdentifierForObject(object)
    guard let cell = tableView.dequeueReusableCellWithIdentifier(
```

```
      identifier , forIndexPath: indexPath) as? Cell
      else { fatalError("Unexpected cell type at \(indexPath)") }
  cell.configureForObject(object)
  return cell
}
```

It also exposes a method, processUpdates(_:), to which we can pass the updates we receive from our fetched results data provider. The details of this are more about UIKit than Core Data, so we'll leave you with this brief description. Of course, you can read the full source code[4] in the sample project.

The final step is to tie all these parts together by implementing the delegate methods of the data provider and the data source:

```
extension MoodsTableViewController: DataProviderDelegate {
    func dataProviderDidUpdate(updates: [DataProviderUpdate<Mood>]?) {
        dataSource.processUpdates(updates)
    }
}

extension MoodsTableViewController: DataSourceDelegate {
    func cellIdentifierForObject(object: Mood) -> String {
        return "MoodCell"
    }
}
```

The first one just passes the updates from the data provider on to the table view data source. The second one simply returns the cell's identifier.

We also need to make our cell class conform to the ConfigurableCell protocol:

```
protocol ConfigurableCell {
    typealias DataSource
    func configureForObject(object: DataSource)
}
```

This is a requirement of our table view data source and allows it to properly configure cells with their underlying data by calling configureForObject(_:) on them. The implementation for MoodTableViewCell is straightforward:

```
extension MoodTableViewCell: ConfigurableCell {
    func configureForObject(mood: Mood) {
        moodView.colors = mood.colors
        label.text = sharedDateFormatter.stringFromDate(mood.date)
        country.text = mood.country?.localizedDescription ?? ""
    }
}
```

We've come pretty far already. We've created the model, set up the Core Data stack, handed the managed object context through the view controller hierarchy, created a fetch request, and hooked up a table view via a fetched results controller to display the data. The only thing missing at this point is actual data that we can display, so let's get onto that.

Manipulating Data

As outlined at the beginning of this chapter, all Core Data managed objects, like instances of our Mood class, live within a managed object context. Therefore, inserting new objects and deleting existing ones is also done via the context. You can think of a managed object context as a scratchpad: none of the changes you make to objects in this context are persisted until you explicitly save them by calling the context's save() method.

Inserting Objects

In our example app, inserting new mood objects is done via taking a new picture with the camera. We won't include all the non-Core Data code here to make this work, but you can check it out on GitHub[5].

When the user snaps a new picture, we insert a new mood object by calling insertNewObjectForEntityName(_:inManagedObjectContext:) on NSEntityDescription, setting the most dominant colors from the image, and then calling save() on the context:

```
guard let mood = NSEntityDescription.insertNewObjectForEntityForName(
    "Mood", inManagedObjectContext: moc) as? Mood
else { fatalError("Wrong object type") }
mood.colors = image.moodColors
```

5 https://github.com/objcio/core-data

```
try! moc.save()
```

However, this is kind of unwieldy code for just inserting an object. First, we
need to downcast the result of the insert call to our Mood type. Second, we
want the colors property to publicly be read-only. Lastly, we potentially have
to handle the error that save() can throw.

We will introduce a few helper methods to clean up the code. As a result, our
code will be much simpler. First, we will add a method to
NSManagedObjectContext to insert new objects without having to manually
downcast the result every time, and without having to reference the entity
type by its name. For this, we leverage the static entityName property that we
introduced in the ManagedObjectType protocol above:

```
extension NSManagedObjectContext {
    public func insertObject<A: ManagedObject where A: ManagedObjectType>
        () -> A
    {
        guard let obj = NSEntityDescription.insertNewObjectForEntityForName(
            A.entityName, inManagedObjectContext: self) as? A
        else { fatalError("Wrong object type") }
        return obj
    }
}
```

This method is defined to be generic over A, which is a subtype of
ManagedObject, and which conforms to the ManagedObjectType protocol. The
compiler can automatically infer the type of the object we're trying to insert
from the type annotation in the call:

```
let mood: Mood = moc.insertObject()
```

Next, we use this new helper in a static method we add to Mood to encapsulate
the object insertion:

```
public final class Mood: ManagedObject {
    // ...
    public static func insertIntoContext(moc: NSManagedObjectContext,
        image: UIImage) -> Mood
    {
        let mood: Mood = moc.insertObject()
        mood.colors = image.moodColors
        mood.date = NSDate()
        return mood
```

```
    }
    // ...
}
```

Finally, we add two more methods to the context to help with saving:

```
extension NSManagedObjectContext {
    public func saveOrRollback() -> Bool {
        do {
            try save()
            return true
        } catch {
            rollback()
            return false
        }
    }

    public func performChanges(block: () -> ()) {
        performBlock {
            block()
            self.saveOrRollback()
        }
    }
}
```

The first one, saveOrRollback(), simply catches the exception that might be thrown from the save() call and rolls back the pending changes in the error case, i.e. it simply abandons the unsaved data. For the example app, this is an acceptable behavior, since conflicts cannot occur in our single managed object context setup. However, depending on your use case, you might want to handle this in more sophisticated ways. The chapter about changing and saving data and the chapter about handling problems with multiple contexts both go into more detail of how to handle save conflicts.

The second one, performChanges(_:), calls performBlock(_:) on the context, calls the block supplied as an argument, and saves the context. The call to performBlock(_:) makes sure that we are on the correct queue to access the context and its managed objects. This will become more relevant when we add a second context that operates on a background queue. For now, just consider it a best practice pattern to always wrap the code that interacts with Core Data objects within such a block.

Now, whenever the user snaps a new picture, we can insert a new mood with a simple three-liner in our root view controller:

```
func didTakeImage(image: UIImage) {
    self.managedObjectContext.performChanges {
        Mood.insertIntoContext(self.managedObjectContext, image: image)
    }
}
```

We can reuse these helper methods all over the project to write cleaner, more readable code — without introducing any magic. Additionally, we've laid a good foundation of best practice patterns that will help us once the application becomes more complex.

Deleting Objects

In order to show how to best handle object deletion, we will add a detail view controller. It will show information about a single *mood* and allow the user to delete that particular mood. We'll expand our example app so that the detail view controller gets pushed onto the navigation stack when you select one of the moods in the table view.

When the segue to this detail view controller occurs, we set the selected mood object as a property on the new view controller:

```
override func prepareForSegue(segue: UIStoryboardSegue, sender: AnyObject?) {
    switch segueIdentifierForSegue(segue) {
    case .ShowMoodDetail:
        guard let vc = segue.destinationViewController
            as? MoodDetailViewController
            else { fatalError("Wrong view controller type") }
        guard let mood = dataSource.selectedObject
            else { fatalError("Showing detail, but no selected row?") }
        vc.mood = mood
    }
}
```

This view controller also has a trash button to delete the mood you're looking at, which triggers the following action:

```
@IBAction func deleteMood(sender: UIBarButtonItem) {
    mood.managedObjectContext?.performChanges {
        self.mood.managedObjectContext?.deleteObject(self.mood)
    }
}
```

To do the actual deletion, we call the previously introduced helper method, performChanges(_:), on the mood's context. We then call the deleteObject(_:) method, with the mood object as argument in the block. The performChanges(_:) helper will take care of saving the context after this operation.

Naturally, it doesn't make sense to have this detail view controller on the stack any longer once the mood itself has been deleted. The most straightforward approach would be to pop the detail view controller from the navigation stack at the same time we delete the mood object. However, we'll take a different approach that is more future-proof — for example, in a situation where the mood object would be deleted in the background as the result of a network syncing operation.

We will use the same approach as the fetched results controller: we will listen to *objects-did-change* notifications. The managed object context posts these notifications to inform you about changes in its managed objects. This way, the desired effect will be the same, no matter what the origin of the change is.

To achieve this, we build a managed object observer, which takes the object to be observed and a closure that will be called whenever the object gets deleted or changed:

```
public final class ManagedObjectObserver {
    public init?(object: ManagedObjectType, changeHandler: ChangeType -> ()) {
        // ...
    }
}
```

In our detail view controller, we initialize the observer like this:

```
private var observer: ManagedObjectObserver?

var mood: Mood! {
    didSet {
        observer = ManagedObjectObserver(object: mood) { [unowned self] type in
            guard type == .Delete else { return }
            self.navigationController?.popViewControllerAnimated(true)
        }
        updateViews()
    }
}
```

We initialize the observer in the **didSet** property observer of the mood property and store it in an instance variable. When the observed mood object gets deleted, the closure gets called with the .Delete change type, and we pop the detail view controller off of the navigation stack. This is a more robust and versatile solution, since we'll be notified of the deletion regardless of whether or not the user caused it directly, or if the deletion came in, for example, via the network in the background.

The ManagedObjectObserver class registers for the *objects-did-change* notification (NSManagedObjectContextObjectsDidChangeNotification), which is sent by Core Data every time changes occur to the managed objects in a context. It registers for the context of the managed object we're interested in, and whenever the notification is sent, it traverses the user info of the notification to check whether or not a deletion of the observed object has occurred:

```
public final class ManagedObjectObserver {
    public enum ChangeType {
        case Delete
        case Update
    }

    public init?(object: ManagedObjectType, changeHandler: ChangeType -> ()) {
        guard let moc = object.managedObjectContext else { return nil }
        objectHasBeenDeleted = !object.dynamicType.defaultPredicate
            .evaluateWithObject(object)
        token = moc.addObjectsDidChangeNotificationObserver {
            [unowned self] note in
            guard let changeType = self.changeTypeOfObject(object,
                inNotification: note)
            else { return }
            self.objectHasBeenDeleted = changeType == .Delete
            changeHandler(changeType)
        }
    }

    deinit {
        NSNotificationCenter.defaultCenter().removeObserver(token)
    }

    private var token: NSObjectProtocol!
    private var objectHasBeenDeleted: Bool = false

    private func changeTypeOfObject(object: ManagedObjectType,
```

```
        inNotification note: ObjectsDidChangeNotification) -> ChangeType?
    {
        let deleted = note.deletedObjects.union(note.invalidatedObjects)
        if note.invalidatedAllObjects ||
            deleted.containsObjectIdenticalTo(object)
        {
            return .Delete
        }
        let updated = note.updatedObjects.union(note.refreshedObjects)
        if updated.containsObjectIdenticalTo(object) {
                return .Update
        }
        return nil
    }
}
```

Whenever the managed object context posts a did-change notification, we
check if all objects have been invalidated or if the observed object is part of the
deleted or invalidated objects. In either case, we call the changeHandler(_:)
closure with the .Delete change type. Similarly, if the object is part of the
updated or refreshed objects, we call the closure with the .Update change type.

There are two interesting things to note in the observer code. First, to observe
the context's notification, we use a strongly typed wrapper around the loosely
typed information of NSNotification's user info dictionary. This makes the
code safer and more readable and encapsulates the typecasting in a central
place. You can look up the full code[6] of this wrapper in the example project on
GitHub.

Second, the containsObjectIdenticalTo(_:) method uses pointer equality
comparison (===) to compare the objects in the set to the observed object. We
can do this because Core Data performs *uniquing*: Core Data guarantees that
there's exactly one single managed object per managed object context for any
entry in the persistent store. We'll go into this in more detail in part two.

Summary

We've covered a lot of ground in this chapter. We created a simple yet
functional example app. Initially, we defined the structure of our data by

---

6 https://github.com/objcio/core-data/blob/master/SharedCode/NSManagedObjectContext+Observers.swift

creating a data model with an entity and its attributes. Then we created a corresponding NSManagedObject subclass for the entity. To set up the Core Data stack, we loaded the data model we defined, created a persistent store coordinator, and added an SQL store to it. Finally, we created the managed object context and set the persistent store coordinator on it.

With the stack in place, we made use of a fetched results controller to load the mood objects from the store and display them in a table view. We also added the functionality for inserting and deleting moods. We used a reactive approach to updating the UI in case the data changes: for the table view, we leveraged Core Data's fetched results controller; and for the detail view, we used our own managed object observer, which is built on top of the context's change notification.

Takeaways

→ Core Data is not just for complex persistency tasks — it can be used equally well for simple projects like the one presented in this chapter.

→ You don't need a code generator to create managed object subclasses; it's very easy to write them by hand for full control.

→ Extend your model classes with a protocol that adds the entity's name, default sort descriptors, and related information, in order to avoid spreading them all over your code.

→ Encapsulate data source and fetched results controller delegate methods into a separate class for code reuse, lean view controllers, and type safety in Swift.

→ Create a few simple helper methods to make your life easier when inserting objects, executing fetch requests, and performing similar repeating tasks.

→ Make sure to update your UI accordingly in case an object that's currently presented gets deleted or changed. We recommend taking a reactive approach to this task: the fetched results controller already handles this for table views, and you can implement a similar pattern by observing the context's did-change notification in other cases.

Relationships

2

In this chapter, we will expand our data model. We will add two new entities: *Country* and *Continent*. During this process, we will explain the concept of subentities and when you should and shouldn't use them. Then we will establish relationships between our three entities. Relationships are a key feature of Core Data, and we will use them to associate each mood with a country, and each country with a continent.

Adding Country and Continent Entities

Changing the data model will cause the app to crash the next time you run it. But as long as you're in the development process and haven't distributed the app, you can simply delete the old version from the device or the simulator, and you're good to go again. In this chapter, we'll assume that we can make changes to the data model without any concerns of breaking existing installations. In the chapter about migrations, we'll discuss how to handle this problem in production.

To create the two new *Country* and *Continent* entities, we go back to Xcode's model editor. Both new entities have a property to store the ISO 3166 code of the country or continent. We call this attribute numericISO3166Code and choose Int16 as data type. Furthermore, both entities have an updatedAt attribute of type NSDate, which we'll use later to sort them in the table view.

The managed object subclass for Country looks like this:

```
public final  class Country: ManagedObject {
    @NSManaged internal var updatedAt: NSDate

    public private(set) var iso3166Code: ISO3166.Country {
        get {
            guard let c = ISO3166.Country(rawValue: numericISO3166Code) else {
                fatalError("Unknown country code")
            }
            return c
        }
        set {
            numericISO3166Code = newValue.rawValue
        }
    }
    @NSManaged private var numericISO3166Code: Int16
}
```

We mark the numericISO3166Code attribute as private, since it's an implementation detail of how a Country object gets persisted. For public use, we add the computed property iso3166Code, which can be set (privately) and read as the ISO3166.Country enum type. This is defined with the three-letter country codes as enum options:

```
public struct ISO3166 {
    public enum Country: Int16 {
        case GUY = 328
        case POL = 616
        case LTU = 440
        //  ...
        case Unknown = 0
    }
}
```

We've also added extensions on this enum to make it printable, to get the continent for a country, etc. You can look up the full enum definition in the sample code[1].

In a very similar fashion, the Continent class is defined as the following:

```
public final  class Continent: ManagedObject {
    @NSManaged internal var updatedAt: NSDate

    public private(set) var iso3166Code: ISO3166.Continent {
        get {
            guard let c = ISO3166.Continent(rawValue: numericISO3166Code)
                else { fatalError("Unknown continent code") }
            return c
        }
        set {
            numericISO3166Code = newValue.rawValue
        }
    }
    @NSManaged private var numericISO3166Code: Int16
}
```

Of course, we also make the Country and Continent classes conform to the ManagedObjectType protocol we introduced in the previous chapter. This way, the new classes benefit from the same convenience functionality we added

1 https://github.com/objcio/core-data/blob/master/Moody/MoodyModel/ISO3166.swift

before, which we can use to insert objects, get preconfigured fetch requests, etc.:

```
extension Country: ManagedObjectType {
    public static var entityName: String {
        return "Country"
    }

    public static var defaultSortDescriptors: [NSSortDescriptor] {
        return [NSSortDescriptor(key: UpdateTimestampKey, ascending: false)]
    }
}

extension Continent: ManagedObjectType {
    public static var entityName: String {
        return "Continent"
    }

    public static var defaultSortDescriptors: [NSSortDescriptor] {
        return [NSSortDescriptor(key: UpdateTimestampKey, ascending: false)]
    }
}
```

Lastly, we introduce a protocol called LocalizedStringConvertible. This has one read-only property: localizedDescription. By making both Country and Continent conform to this protocol, we'll have a unified way to configure a label with a region's name later on:

```
extension Country: LocalizedStringConvertible {
    public var localizedDescription: String {
        return iso3166Code.localizedDescription
    }
}

extension Continent: LocalizedStringConvertible {
    public var localizedDescription: String {
        return iso3166Code.localizedDescription
    }
}
```

Since we only store the country's ISO code, we can use NSLocale to show the localized name of the country. For continents, we'd have to provide this localization ourselves.

Next up is associating a mood with a country it was taken in. In order to do this, we also want to store the geolocation with each mood. We'll add two new attributes to the *Mood* entity: latitude and longitude, both of type Double, and both optional, since location data might not be available. We could have stored a CLLocation object in a transformable attribute, but that would be rather wasteful, since there's much more data associated with it than what we need. Instead, we store the raw latitude and longitude values and expose a location property on the Mood class, which constructs a CLLocation from those values:

```
public final class Mood: ManagedObject {
    // ...
    public var location: CLLocation? {
        guard let lat = latitude, lon = longitude else { return nil }
        return CLLocation(latitude: lat.doubleValue, longitude: lon.doubleValue)
    }
    @NSManaged private var latitude: NSNumber?
    @NSManaged private var longitude: NSNumber?
    // ...
}
```

We have to represent the latitude and longitude attributes as NSNumber properties in the Mood class, because we want them to be optional. We'd prefer to declare the property as Double?, but this type cannot be represented in Objective-C and therefore does not work with the **@NSManaged** annotation.

Subentities

The entities in a model can be organized hierarchically: an entity can be a subentity of another, inheriting the attributes and relationships of the parent entity. While this sounds similar to subclassing, it is important to understand the difference.

The only reason to create subentities is when you need to have different object types in the result of a single fetch request or in a relationship. In our case, we want to show a table view that displays either both countries and continents mixed together or just one of them at a time. We can achieve this by adding an abstract *GeographicRegion* entity and making *Continent* and *Country* a subentity of these. Since *Continent* and *Country* share the same attributes (numericISO3166Code and updatedAt), we can move them into their abstract parent entity:

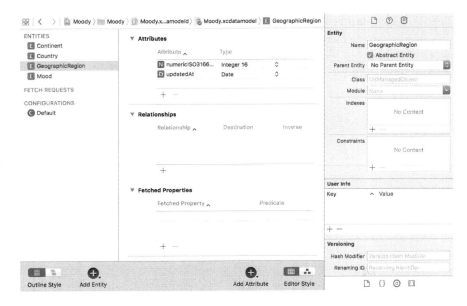

Figure 2.1: The abstract *GeographicRegion* parent entity in Xcode's model editor

For this, we'd be able to create a fetch request for the *GeographicRegion* entity, and it would return both countries and continents. Note, however, that introducing the abstract parent entity has not changed the way we set up the managed object subclasses at all. There's no common GeographicRegion superclass for Country and Continent. There could be if it would make sense for our use case, but there doesn't have to be. The class hierarchy and the entity hierarchy are independent of one another:

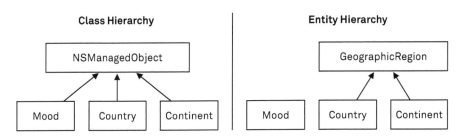

Figure 2.2: The NSManagedObject class hierarchy doesn't have to match up with the entity hierarchy

Understanding and Avoiding Subentities

Quite often, you'll end up with a model where multiple entities share a common set of attributes (e.g. IDs or timestamps). It may be tempting to create a parent entity and add all the common attributes there only once, but that has dramatic consequences. Subentities of a common parent entity will share a common database table, and all attributes of all sibling entities are combined into this one table, even though Core Data hides this on the level you're interacting with. This will quickly become a performance and memory problem, because Core Data has to read everything from one giant database table. (If you're not familiar with the structure of relational databases, check out the chapter about relational database basics and SQL.)

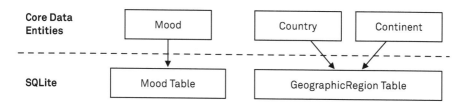

Figure 2.3: How Core Data collapses subentities into a common SQLite table

It's useful to think of subentities as a fancy way of adding a "type" enum (an enum that tells you if the given instance is of type "A" or "B") to a single entity. When you wonder whether or not to use subentities, perform the following thought experiment: Would it feel very wrong to collapse all entities with a common parent into a single entity with a type attribute? If it does, you shouldn't use subentities.

Unless you need to have multiple types of objects in the same fetch request result, or in the same relationship, it's best to avoid using subentities. Note that it is perfectly acceptable for multiple classes to share a common superclass without them being subentities of the same entity. However, instead of subclassing, it's probably better to use a common protocol in Swift.

An example of this is the LocalizedStringConvertible protocol above, which is implemented both by Country and Continent. Using a protocol allows us to treat them as the same thing with regard to displaying their localized names — without sharing a common superclass. Similarly, you could define a protocol for common properties on all of your managed object classes — for example, a remote ID or timestamp property.

Creating Relationships

A central and very powerful feature of Core Data is its ability to manage relationships. We will create relationships between all three of our entities.

We want to be able to show the user a list of geographic regions (in a table view). If the user selects a country, we will show the moods taken in that country. If the user selects a continent, we will show all moods taken in any country on that continent. Additionally, we want to be able to filter this list of regions to show only countries or continents.

The relationships are such that a continent has multiple countries, while each country belongs to one continent (at least in our simplified view of the world). Each country can have multiple moods, while each mood is in one country. The relationships in this example are so-called *one-to-many* relationships.

What we call a one-to-many relationship really consists of two relationships in the model: one in each direction. To establish the relationship between Continent and Country, we really define two relationships in the model editor: one from Continent to Country, and one from Country to Continent. The relationship on Continent is called countries (plural, since it's to-many), and the relationship on Country is called continent (singular, since it's to-one). Similarly, we set up a to-many relationship called moods, from Country to Mood, as well as a to-one relationship called country, from Mood to Country:

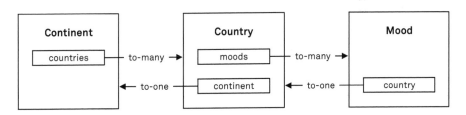

Figure 2.4: The relationships between the *Continent*, *Country*, and *Mood* entities

Core Data will automatically keep the inverse relationship up to date: when we set the continent on a Country, the countries property on the corresponding Continent is automatically updated, and vice versa. Note that the update of the inverse relationship doesn't happen right away, but rather when processPendingChanges() is called on the context. You don't have to do this manually; Core Data will take care of this at the appropriate times. See the chapter about changing and saving data for more details.

We will add these relationships to our managed object subclasses as well:

```
public final class Mood: ManagedObject {
    // ...
    @NSManaged public private(set) var country: Country
    // ...
}

public final class Country: ManagedObject {
    // ...
    @NSManaged private(set) var moods: Set<Mood>
    @NSManaged private(set) var continent: Continent?
    // ...
}

public final class Continent: ManagedObject {
    // ...
    @NSManaged public private(set) var countries: Set<Country>
    // ...
}
```

You might have noticed that the continent relationship on Country is marked as optional. That's because moods without location data will be associated with an "unknown" country (we've defined an Unknown case in the ISO3166.Country enum), and this unknown country does not belong to any continent.

> You don't *have* to add the relationships defined in the data model to your NSManagedObject subclasses. We do that here because we want to use them in our code. But Core Data would work just fine if the classes wouldn't have the inverse relationship defined, as long as it's defined in the data model.

Other Types of Relationships

In the example above, we only used one-to-many relationships. However, often you want to create a relationship between two entities that is either *one-to-one* or *many-to-many*. Core Data supports all this and more out of the box.

Creating a one-to-one relationship is very similar to what we did for the one-to-many relationships above: create the relationship and its inverse, but this time, set the relationship type to *to-one* on both ends. Similarly, a many-to-many relationship is created by setting the relationships in both directions to *to-many*. As with one-to-many relationships, Core Data will automatically keep the reverse relationship up to date in the one-to-one and the many-to-many cases.

Under the hood, many-to-many relationships are more complicated in the SQL backing store than one-to-one or one-to-many relationships. They use a join table. The chapter on relational database basics and SQL goes into more detail on this.

Ordered Relationships

To-many relationships come in two flavors: unordered and ordered. By default, to-many relationships don't have a particular order, as can be seen by their data type. Standard to-many relationships are represented by properties of type Set (NSSet in Objective-C). This guarantees uniqueness of the contained objects, but no particular order.

When you select a to-many relationship in the model editor, you can activate the *ordered* checkbox in the data model inspector to change this default behavior. Ordered relationships are represented by NSOrderedSet properties, which guarantee uniqueness *and* a specific order of the contained elements. See the section below about mutating to-many relationships to learn how to best insert and remove objects in an ordered relationship.

> The underlying mechanism Core Data uses to persist the order of the objects of an ordered relationship is an opaque implementation detail. However, we can still retrieve those objects in the same sort order as in the ordered relationship by using a fetch request: just specify the name of the ordered relationship's inverse as sort key of a sort descriptor.

Other Use Cases

Relationships don't always have to be between two different entities. You can also establish a relationship from an entity to itself — for example, to build up a tree structure by adding parent and children relationships to the same entity.

Another non-obvious use case is to establish multiple relationships between two entities. For example, you could have a *Country* and a *Person* entity, where there are multiple ways of how persons can be associated with countries. For example, a person could be citizen and resident of the same country or of different countries. We would model this as one-to-many relationships called residents and citizens, with inverse relationships called residentOf and citizenOf, respectively.

Finally, you can also create unidirectional relationships, i.e. relationships that don't have a corresponding inverse relationship. However, you should be *very* careful with this, since it can lead to referential integrity problems in your dataset. This means that one entry in the database might point to another entry that doesn't exist anymore. This can happen when you delete an object that's referred to by other objects but doesn't have a relationship back to those objects. Normally, Core Data ensures that relationships are updated properly when objects are deleted. Once you use unidirectional relationships, you have to do this yourself.

You should only think about using unidirectional relationships if you're entirely sure that you will never delete an object that's missing its inverse relationship. Consider this example: we have a *Message* entity and a *User* entity that are related by a sender to-one relationship from *Message* to *User*. If we're absolutely sure that we'll never delete User objects, we might consider leaving out the inverse messages relationship from *User* to *Message* to avoid the overhead of updating this relationship, since we'll never use it. But be aware that this can be a typical case of premature optimization — be sure to first check whether this is a performance problem at all.

Establishing Relationships

In our case, we want to set the mood's country when the mood is created, and we want to set a country's continent when the country is created. For the former, we modify the static convenience method on the Mood class to set the country:

```
public static func insertIntoContext(moc: NSManagedObjectContext,
    image: UIImage, location: CLLocation?, placemark: CLPlacemark?) -> Mood
{
    let mood: Mood = moc.insertObject()
    mood.colors = image.moodColors
    mood.date = NSDate()
    if let coord = location?.coordinate {
        mood.latitude = coord.latitude
        mood.longitude = coord.longitude
    }
    let isoCode = placemark?.ISOcountryCode ?? ""
    let isoCountry = ISO3166.Country.fromISO3166(isoCode)
    mood.country = Country.findOrCreateCountry(isoCountry, inContext: moc)
    return mood
}
```

After we've converted the placemark's country code to an ISO3166.Country value (which will be .Unknown if the code is not recognized), we get the corresponding country object by calling findOrCreateCountry(_:inContext:) on the Country class. This helper method checks if the country already exists, and then creates it if it doesn't:

```
static func findOrCreateCountry(isoCountry: ISO3166.Country,
    inContext moc: NSManagedObjectContext) -> Country
{
    let predicate = NSPredicate(format: "%K == %d",
        Keys.NumericISO3166Code.rawValue, Int(isoCountry.rawValue))
    let country = findOrCreateInContext(moc, matchingPredicate: predicate) {
        $0.iso3166Code = isoCountry
        $0.continent = Continent.findOrCreateContinentForCountry(isoCountry,
            inContext: moc)
    }
    return country
}
```

The heavy lifting is done by the findOrCreateInContext(_:matchingPredicate:) method that's defined in an extension to the ManagedObjectType protocol:

```
extension ManagedObjectType where Self: ManagedObject {
    public static func findOrCreateInContext(moc: NSManagedObjectContext,
        matchingPredicate predicate: NSPredicate,
        configure: Self -> ())  -> Self
    {
        guard let obj = findOrFetchInContext(moc,
            matchingPredicate: predicate) else
```

```
    {
        let newObject: Self = moc.insertObject()
        configure(newObject)
        return newObject
    }
    return obj
}

public static func findOrFetchInContext(moc: NSManagedObjectContext,
    matchingPredicate predicate: NSPredicate) -> Self?
{
    guard let obj = materializedObjectInContext(moc,
        matchingPredicate: predicate)
    else {
        return fetchInContext(moc) { request in
            request.predicate = predicate
            request.returnsObjectsAsFaults = false
            request.fetchLimit = 1
        }. first
    }
    return obj
}
}
```

Let's go through this step by step: first, we call the
findOrFetchInContext(_:matchingPredicate:) helper method. Here, we check if
the object we're looking for is already registered in the context. This step is a
performance optimization — in our case, chances are good that we've already
loaded the country object into memory before. Even traversing a large array of
in-memory objects is way faster than executing a fetch request, which round
trips all the way to the file system. We'll talk more about this aspect in the
performance chapter.

If we don't find the object in the context, we try to load it using a fetch request.
In case the object already exists in Core Data, it will be returned by the fetch
request. If it doesn't exist yet, we create a new object and give the caller of this
helper method a chance to configure the newly created object.

The code above uses two more helper methods on our ManagedObjectType
protocol that are worth noting:
materializedObjectInContext(_:matchingPredicate:) iterates over the context's
registeredObjects set, which contains all managed objects the context
currently knows about. It does this until it finds one that is not a fault, is of the
correct type, and matches a given predicate:

```
extension ManagedObjectType where Self: ManagedObject {
    public static func materializedObjectInContext(
        moc: NSManagedObjectContext,
        matchingPredicate predicate: NSPredicate) -> Self?
    {
        for obj in moc.registeredObjects where !obj.fault {
            guard let res = obj as? Self
                where predicate.evaluateWithObject(res)
                else { continue }
            return res
        }
        return nil
    }
}
```

The important aspect here is that we only consider objects that are not faults in the iteration. A fault is a managed object instance that's not populated with data yet (see the chapter about accessing data for more details). If we would try to evaluate our predicate on faults, we'd potentially force Core Data to make a round trip to the persistent store for each fault, in order to fill in the missing data — something that could be very expensive.

The second helper method on ManagedObjectType makes it easier to execute fetch requests. It combines the configuration and the execution of a fetch request. It also casts the result to the correct type:

```
extension ManagedObjectType where Self: ManagedObject {
    public static func fetchInContext(context: NSManagedObjectContext,
        @noescape configurationBlock: NSFetchRequest -> () = { _ in })
        -> [Self]
    {
        let request = NSFetchRequest(entityName: Self.entityName)
        configurationBlock(request)
        guard let result = try! context.executeFetchRequest(request)
            as? [Self]
            else { fatalError("Fetched objects have wrong type") }
        return result
    }
}
```

Now, let's return to what we were trying to accomplish before this excursion. We already extended the static helper method on Mood to set the country relationship by either looking up an existing country object or by creating a new one. In the latter case, a continent has to be set on the new country object.

We retrieve this continent object in exactly the same way as we did above for the country:

```swift
static func findOrCreateContinentForCountry(isoCountry: ISO3166.Country,
    inContext moc: NSManagedObjectContext) -> Continent?
{
    guard let iso3166 = ISO3166.Continent.fromCountry(isoCountry)
        else { return nil }
    let predicate = NSPredicate(format: "%K == %d",
        Keys.NumericISO3166Code.rawValue, Int(iso3166.rawValue))
    let continent = findOrCreateInContext(moc,
        matchingPredicate: predicate) { $0.iso3166Code = iso3166 }
    return continent
}
```

Mutating To-Many Relationships

In our example above, we only establish relationships from the to-one side of our one-to-many relationships by simply setting the object on the other side on the relationship property. Of course, you can also mutate a relationship from the other end, i.e. change what's in the to-many side of the relationship. The most straightforward way to do this is to get a mutable set for the relationship property and make the change you want.

For example, we could add the following private property on the Country class to mutate the moods relationship (we don't need this in our example but will include it for the sake of demonstration):

```swift
private var mutableMoods: NSMutableSet {
    return mutableSetValueForKey(Keys.Moods)
}
```

The moods relationship is still exposed as an immutable set to the rest of the world, but internally we can use this mutable version to, for example, add a new mood object:

```swift
mutableMoods.addObject(mood)
```

The same approach works for ordered to-many relationships as well. You just have to use mutableOrderedSetValueForKey(_:) instead of mutableSetValueForKey(_:).

It's worth noting that the Xcode NSManagedObject subclass generator creates helper methods that actually don't work on ordered relationships. But as we've just seen, that shouldn't stop you from using ordered relationships. Using the mutable (ordered) set accessors is the recommended and often easier approach anyway.

Relationships and Deletion

Relationships play a special role during deletion: when you delete an object that has a relationship to another object, you have to decide what should happen to the related object. For example, when a country object is deleted, Core Data needs to update the countries relationship on the corresponding continent object to reflect the change. To achieve this, we set the delete rule for the country's continent relationship to *nullify*. This causes the related object — in our example, the continent — to stay around, with its reverse relationship, countries, being updated:

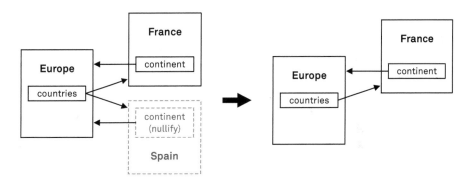

Figure 2.5: The *nullify* delete rule removes the deleted object from its inverse relationship

The delete rule can also be set to *cascade*, which causes the object(s) at the other end to be deleted too. Although we don't do this in our specific example, it could make sense to adopt this rule for the countries relationship on Continent. For example, when a continent object gets deleted, we might want Core Data to delete all associated country objects as well:

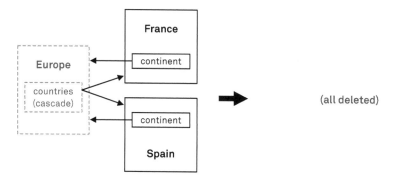

Figure 2.6: The *cascade* delete rule propagates the deletion to related objects

We actually want to guarantee that continent and country objects are not deleted, as long as they have any associated country or mood objects, respectively. Core Data has another delete rule to enforce this: *deny*. Setting the delete rule to deny on the continent's countries relationship will cause the deletion of a continent object to fail if it still has associated countries:

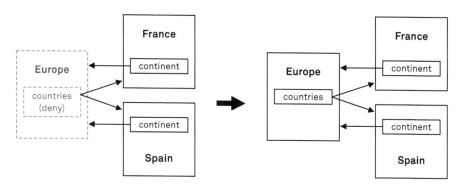

Figure 2.7: The *deny* delete rule prevents deletion of the object if the relationship is not empty

The last delete rule, *no action*, should be used with care: this means that Core Data will not update the inverse relationship(s), but we as the developers promise Core Data that we have put some custom code in place to update the inverse relationship(s) ourselves.

Custom Delete Rules

Sometimes you want a different delete propagation behavior than what's possible with using Core Data's delete rules. For example, in our case, we want to clean up country objects that don't reference moods any longer, as well as continent objects that don't reference countries anymore. We can achieve this by hooking into the prepareForDeletion() method in the Country class:

```
public final class Country: ManagedObject {
    // ...
    public override func prepareForDeletion() {
        guard let c = continent else { return }
        if c.countries.filter ({ !$0.deleted }).isEmpty {
            managedObjectContext?.deleteObject(c)
        }
    }
    // ...
}
```

This method will be called just before the object is deleted. Here, we can check if the continent's countries relationship still contains non-deleted countries. If it doesn't, we delete the continent. We can use the same approach in the Mood class to delete country objects that no longer reference any moods.

Adapting the User Interface

To show the countries and continents in the UI, we add another table view controller. We'll insert this controller into the navigation stack before the controller that displays the mood objects. This table view will display the countries and the continents in one combined list. Additionally, it has an option to filter the list to only show either continents or countries:

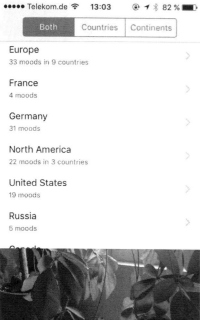

Figure 2.8: The regions table view in the sample app

In this table view controller, we use the same generic data provider and data source classes that we introduced in the last chapter for the moods table view. We set this up by calling the following method from the region table view controller's viewDidLoad():

```
private func setupDataSource() {
    let  request = filterSegmentedControl.regionFilter.fetchRequest
    let  frc  = NSFetchedResultsController(fetchRequest: request,
        managedObjectContext: managedObjectContext,
        sectionNameKeyPath: nil, cacheName: nil)
    let  dataProvider = FetchedResultsDataProvider(
        fetchedResultsController: frc, delegate: self)
    dataSource = TableViewDataSource(tableView: tableView,
        dataProvider: dataProvider, delegate: self)
}
```

The interesting part here is how we create the fetch request for the selected segment in the top bar. In the moods table view controller, we simply used our convenience property, sortedFetchRequest, on the Mood class. But now the situation is different: we want to show objects of either the *Country* or *Continent* entity, or both at the same time.

We start by creating an enum that represents the different filtering options the user can select in the segmented control:

```
private enum RegionFilter: Int {
    case Both = 0
    case Countries = 1
    case Continents = 2
}
```

Then we add an extension to UISegmentedControl (which we use to select which kind of regions should be shown). This returns a RegionFilter value, depending on its selection index:

```
extension UISegmentedControl {
    private var regionFilter: RegionFilter {
        guard let rf = RegionFilter(rawValue: selectedSegmentIndex) else {
            fatalError("Invalid filter index")
        }
        return rf
    }
}
```

Finally, we extend the RegionFilter enum to add a fetchRequest property, which returns the appropriate fetch request for the current selection:

```
extension RegionFilter {
    var fetchRequest: NSFetchRequest {
        var request: NSFetchRequest
        switch self {
        case .Both: request = GeographicRegion.sortedFetchRequest
        case .Countries: request = Country.sortedFetchRequest
        case .Continents: request = Continent.sortedFetchRequest
        }
        request.returnsObjectsAsFaults = false
        request.fetchBatchSize = 20
        return request
    }
}
```

This is straightforward for the Countries and Continents cases, but the Both case can't work yet — we haven't even defined a GeographicRegion type. To fetch both countries and continents with one fetch request, we can specify their abstract parent entity, *GeographicRegion*, which we created in our data model. In order to be able to call GeographicRegion.sortedFetchRequest in the same way we do with Country and Continent, we define a GeographicRegion type that conforms to the ManagedObjectType protocol:

```
public class GeographicRegion: ManagedObject {}

extension GeographicRegion: ManagedObjectType {
    public static var entityName: String { return "GeographicRegion" }

    public static var defaultSortDescriptors: [NSSortDescriptor] {
        return [NSSortDescriptor(key: "updatedAt", ascending: false)]
    }
}
```

Now we don't have to make an exception for this case, and the entity name is nicely encapsulated.

Moving on, let's implement the cellIdentifierForObject(_:) delegate method of our generic data source. Since the table view displays objects of different types, Country and Continent, the question of how we should specify the Object type alias in the delegate protocol arises. We could use NSManagedObject and then try to cast the objects to Country or Continent to figure out what we're dealing with. But we'll take a different approach here that will simplify the delegate code by introducing another protocol:

```
protocol DisplayableRegion: LocalizedStringConvertible {
    var reuseIdentifier: String { get }
    var localizedDetailDescription: String { get }
    var segue: RegionsTableViewController.SegueIdentifier { get }
}
```

We make Country and Continent conform to this protocol by implementing the reuseIdentifier and segue properties:

```
extension DisplayableRegion {
    var reuseIdentifier: String { return "Region" }
}

extension Country: DisplayableRegion {
    var localizedDetailDescription: String {
```

```
        return localized(.Regions_numberOfMoods, args: [numberOfMoods])
    }
    var segue: RegionsTableViewController.SegueIdentifier {
        return .ShowCountryMoods
    }
}

extension Continent: DisplayableRegion {
    var localizedDetailDescription: String {
        return localized(.Regions_numberOfMoodsInCountries,
            args: [numberOfMoods, numberOfCountries])
    }
    var segue: RegionsTableViewController.SegueIdentifier {
        return .ShowContinentMoods
    }
}
```

Additionally, we implement the ConfigurableCell protocol in an extension on RegionTableViewCell, just as we did in the previous chapter for the mood cell:

```
extension RegionTableViewCell: ConfigurableCell {
    func configureForObject(object: DisplayableRegion) {
        titleLabel.text = object.localizedDescription
        detailLabel.text = object.localizedDetailDescription
    }
}
```

With this in place, the data source delegate method is straightforward:

```
extension RegionsTableViewController: DataSourceDelegate {
    func cellIdentifierForObject(object: DisplayableRegion) -> String {
        return object.reuseIdentifier
    }
}
```

In the full sample project, we go one step further and add an extra "All Moods" row to the beginning of the regions table view. To make this possible, we've added another data provider class that builds on top of FetchedResultsDataProvider and allows us to specify supplementary rows, which are not part of the fetch result, via its delegate. You can check out the code for this on GitHub[2].

---

2 https://github.com/objcio/core-data/blob/master/Moody/Moody/AugmentedFetchedResultsDataProvider.swift

Summary

In this chapter, we added two new entities, *Country* and *Continent*, and established relationships between them: a continent has one or more countries, and a country has one or more moods. We defined those relationships in both directions, e.g. from country to mood, and from mood to country. When we establish or break a relationship between two objects, Core Data will automatically update the inverse relationship. Furthermore, Core Data will also propagate or prevent deletions of objects related to other objects based on the delete rules we set on the relationships.

With those new entities and relationships in place, we updated our convenience method to insert new moods, so that the corresponding country and continent will automatically be created if they don't exist yet. As a performance optimization, we first iterate over the objects registered with the context to check if a country or continent already exists before we fall back to a slower fetch request.

Takeaways

→ Only use subentities if you can reasonably collapse them into one entity with an enum attribute.

→ Core Data can handle one-to-one, one-to-many, and many-to-many relationships.

→ To-many relationships come in two flavors: unordered and ordered.

→ An entity can have a relationship to itself, e.g. a parent attribute to create a tree structure.

→ Two entities can be connected by multiple relationships.

→ Make sure to set the appropriate delete rules on the relationships for your use case.

→ Use the mutableSetForKey(_:) or mutableOrderedSetForKey(_:) accessors to mutate to-many relationships.

Data Types

3

In this chapter, we'll take a more detailed look at the data types Core Data supports out of the box. We'll also address how to store custom data types in different ways involving tradeoffs between convenience, data size, and performance.

Standard Data Types

Core Data supports a number of built-in data types out of the box: integer and floating-point values, booleans, strings, dates, and binary data. Below, we'll look at those types and address some points you should keep in mind when using them.

Numeric Types

Numbers come in various formats: 16-, 32-, and 64-bit integers; single- and double-precision floating-point values; and decimal numbers for base-10 arithmetic. The boolean and date types are also backed by numbers. Booleans are stored as either 0 or 1.

The numeric type you choose to store number values depends on the range of numbers) you have to store. For example, if you know that you will only have to store small numbers (e.g. between -32,768 and +32,767), a 16-bit integer is enough and will both save space in the database and make fetching the data more efficient. For floating-point values, we recommend always using double precision unless there's a good reason not to. Decimal numbers are mostly used for dealing with currency values.

The numeric type you choose for an attribute in the model editor has to match the type you use for the corresponding property in the NSManagedObject subclass. For example, if you choose a 16-bit integer in the model editor, your property has to be defined as Int16. The same applies to floating-point types, i.e. single- and double-precision attributes have to be represented as Float and Double, respectively.

When you write your managed object subclass in Objective-C, you can either use NSNumber properties for all numeric attributes (integers and floating-point values of all sizes), or, often more conveniently, declare the properties using the appropriate scalar types: int16_t, int32_t, int64_t, float, or double.

Decimal numbers are represented by NSDecimalNumber in both Swift and Objective-C. If you're storing currency values, you should probably take a close look at this option. NSDecimalNumber lets you specify exactly how numbers are rounded and how to handle exactness, overflow, and underflow.

Dates

NSDate is simply a wrapper around a double-precision "time interval since reference date," i.e. seconds since January 1, 2001, at midnight UTC. And when Core Data stores a date, it simply stores this double-precision value in the database. NSDate values do not have a time zone, so if you need to store time zone information, you have to add a separate attribute for it. However, in most cases, just storing the NSDate should be enough. You can then use the user's current time zone whenever you want to display the date in the UI.

Binary Data

Storing binary data (i.e. NSData) in an attribute is very straightforward. It can be used directly (for things like JPEG data) or indirectly (for implementing custom data types, as outlined below).

Core Data supports so-called *external storage* for binary values by setting the allowsExternalBinaryDataStorage property on an NSAttributeDescription instance, or by enabling the "Allows External Storage" checkbox in the Data Model Inspector. This lets Core Data decide whether it stores binary data within SQLite or as external files, based on the size of the data. The underlying SQLite database can efficiently store binary data up to roughly 100 kilobytes[1] directly in the database. This option should generally be enabled.

Keep in mind that including large binary data in your model objects will make them more expensive to keep in memory. If, in most cases, you need the binary data together with the other attributes in the entity, it makes sense to store them together. Otherwise, it might be worthwhile to store the binary data in a separate entity and create a relationship between the two.

Another alternative is to only store file names in Core Data and manage the storage of the actual data on disk yourself. However, you should have a very good reason to do this instead of just storing the data in Core Data itself. You're

---

1 https://www.sqlite.org/intern-v-extern-blob.html

taking on full responsibility to ensure data integrity between Core Data and your own binary storage, which is not always an easy task.

Strings

Adding a string attribute works as you'd expect: the string is stored with full Unicode support. Unfortunately, searching and sorting by strings can be quite complex. That's not Core Data's fault though; it's just inherently difficult due to the complexity of Unicode itself and the different expectations of what constitutes correct behavior based on language. For more on this, we have an entire chapter dedicated to advanced string topics.

Primitive Properties and Transient Attributes

Before we discuss the different approaches to storing custom data types, we'll briefly explain the concepts of primitive properties and transient attributes. We'll need those concepts later on when we talk about implementing accessor methods for custom data types.

Primitive Properties

In an NSManagedObject subclass, Core Data dynamically implements the setter and getter methods for the properties representing the entity's attributes. That's why we mark the declarations of those properties with **@NSManaged** in Swift: this tells the compiler that Core Data will supply the accessor methods at runtime. Those accessor methods take care of all the Core Data-specific tasks, like faulting in data from the store, keeping track of changes, etc.

Next to those public-facing properties, Core Data also implements a so-called *primitive property* for each attribute. Primitive properties use a primitive prefix in the name, followed by the name of the attribute, starting with an uppercase letter. For example, for a date property, the primitive variant would be primitiveDate. In order to use those properties in our custom classes, we have to declare them with the same **@NSManaged** attribute. You should also always add the **private** keyword to those declarations, since primitive properties are an implementation detail of a particular managed object subclass.

Primitive properties basically exist as a backing store for the Core Data attributes. You should never access them directly other than for the purpose of implementing your own custom accessor methods, as we'll discuss in more detail below.

Transient Attributes

Transient attributes are attributes that are not persisted. The data of a transient attribute is lost when the managed object turns into a fault or ceases to exist altogether. You can mark any attribute as transient in the data model inspector and thus turn it into an attribute that is in-memory only.

The advantage of using transient attributes over normal (non-**@NSManaged**) properties is that they participate in Core Data's change tracking and faulting process. For example, when a managed object turns into a fault, the data of the transient attribute will be thrown away as well (more on faulting in the next chapter). This way, you don't run into the danger of in-memory properties getting out of sync with properties backed by Core Data.

Generally, you should always use transient attributes if you need additional, non-persisted properties in your managed object subclasses. Of course, this doesn't apply to *computed* properties that don't have storage of their own.

Custom Data Types

Aside from the default data types, you can also store custom data types in Core Data. We've already seen an example of this: the colors attribute on the *Mood* entity of type "Transformable." Transformable attributes work out of the box for data types that conform to NSCoding. However, you can also specify a custom value transformer to store your data in a more efficient format.

In any case, it's important that your custom data types are immutable value types. You need to set a new value whenever the data changes. Only then can Core Data pick up the change and persist it during the next save. Put differently, if you would set a mutable object on a Core Data property and then change a piece of data within this mutable object, Core Data would be unable to track this change. In turn, it would lead to undefined behavior and possibly data loss.

Custom Value Transformers

In this section, we'll implement a more efficient way of storing the colors attribute on the *Mood* entity. In the first chapter, we simply used a transformable attribute, since both NSArray and UIColor already conform to NSCoding. The drawback of this approach is that it's wasting quite a bit of space in the database, and it's not the most performant implementation either, since the data will be stored in the property list format.

We can store this data more efficiently by providing our own value transformer, which will store the array of colors as a simple sequence of red, green, and blue values, only requiring three bytes per color. (We don't need the alpha channel in our example.)

The first step is to create two functions that convert an array of colors to NSData, and vice versa. For this purpose, we'll add computed properties on [UIColor] and NSData. Let's first take a look at the conversion from [UIColor] to NSData:

```
extension SequenceType where Generator.Element == UIColor {
    public var moodData: NSData {
        let rgbValues = flatMap { $0.rgb }
        return rgbValues.withUnsafeBufferPointer {
            return NSData(bytes: $0.baseAddress, length: $0.count)
        }
    }
}
```

First, the array of UIColor objects is transformed into an array of UInt8; to do so, it uses this rgb helper on UIColor:

```
extension UIColor {
    private var rgb: [UInt8] {
        var red: CGFloat = 0
        var green: CGFloat = 0
        var blue: CGFloat = 0
        getRed(&red, green: &green, blue: &blue, alpha: nil)
        return [UInt8(red * 255), UInt8(green * 255), UInt8(blue * 255)]
    }
}
```

Next, we convert this array of unsigned 8-bit integers to NSData by using Swift's withUnsafeBufferPointer(_:) helper. This method takes a closure as argument, which will be called with an UnsafeBufferPointer that we can use to create an NSData instance.

For the other direction, from NSData to [UIColor], the transform function looks like this:

```
extension NSData {
    public var moodColors: [UIColor]? {
        guard length > 0 && length % 3 == 0 else { return nil }
        var rgbValues = Array(count: length, repeatedValue: UInt8())
        rgbValues.withUnsafeMutableBufferPointer { buffer -> () in
            let voidPointer = UnsafeMutablePointer<Void>(buffer.baseAddress)
            memcpy(voidPointer, bytes, length)
        }
        let rgbSlices = rgbValues.slices(3)
        return rgbSlices.map { slice in
            guard let color = UIColor(rawData: slice) else {
                fatalError("cannot fail  since we know tuple is of length 3")
            }
            return color
        }
    }
}
```

This is a bit more complicated. First, we have to check if the data is valid at all, i.e. if it has a number of elements divisible by three. If it's valid, we create the rgbValues array of type [UInt8] with the right size to hold all bytes contained in the data object. Then we call withUnsafeMutableBufferPointer(_:) on this array and copy over the data from NSData's buffer to the buffer we get in the closure. The rest is easy, as we slice the array up into arrays of three and map those slices to UIColor objects using the following convenience initializer on UIColor:

```
extension UIColor {
    private convenience init?(rawData: [UInt8]) {
        if  rawData.count != 3 { return nil }
        let red = CGFloat(rawData[0]) / 255
        let green = CGFloat(rawData[1]) / 255
        let blue = CGFloat(rawData[2]) / 255
        self.init(red: red, green: green, blue: blue, alpha: 1)
    }
}
```

With those transformer methods in place, we can create a function to register a value transformer named "ColorsTransformer":

```
private var registrationToken: dispatch_once_t = 0
private let ColorsTransformerName = "ColorsTransformer"

extension Mood {
    static func registerValueTransformers() {
        dispatch_once(&registrationToken) {
            ValueTransformer.registerTransformerWithName(
                ColorsTransformerName, transform:
            { colors in
                guard let colors = colors as? [UIColor] else { return nil }
                return colors.moodData
            }, reverseTransform: { (data: NSData?) -> NSArray? in
                return data?.moodColors
            })
        }
    }
}
```

Here we use a generic, closure-based wrapper around NSValueTransformer to benefit from a strongly typed interface. You can look up the full source code for this on GitHub[2].

Next, we call this registration method when we initialize the Core Data stack:

```
public func createMoodyMainContext() -> NSManagedObjectContext {
    Mood.registerValueTransformers()
    // ...
}
```

Lastly, we open the *Mood* entity in the model editor and set the transformer name of the colors attribute to "ColorsTransformer". From now on, our color data will be stored as a very compact and efficient binary blob:

2 https://github.com/objcio/core-data/blob/master/SharedCode/ValueTransformer.swift

Figure 3.1: Setting the name of the custom value transformer in the Data Model Inspector

Whether or not all this is worth the effort is something you have to judge for your specific use case. If you are storing a lot of custom data and you can easily store it in a more space-efficient manner, it's a nice attention to detail on mobile devices that are sometimes space constrained.

Custom Accessor Methods

Above, we used a transformable attribute in combination with a custom value transformer to implement our own way of storing an array of colors. But there's another way we can achieve this with a different set of tradeoffs: we can create an internal attribute with a standard data type as persistent storage and then add a transient (i.e. a non-persisted) attribute, for which we implement our own accessor methods, which will be exposed publicly.

The main advantage of this approach is that we can lazily do the transformation from the stored raw data to the custom data structure. With a transformable attribute, the transformation happens as soon as a managed object is populated with data. However, if we know that we won't need to access this property most of the time, and the transformation is not cheap, it can make sense to defer it until the data is actually needed. For our use case of storing the color array, using a transformable attribute is perfectly fine. Nevertheless, we will show you the alternative implementation here.

We start by adding a new attribute to the *Mood* entity called colorStorage of type binary data. Then we add the corresponding property to the Mood class:

@NSManaged private var colorStorage: NSData

We mark this property as private because it's an implementation detail the rest of the world doesn't need to know about. Next, we change the type of the colors attribute from transformable to undefined, and we also check the "Transient" checkbox in the data model inspector. Transient attributes are not saved to the persistent store; they only exist while the object is alive. Yet they still participate in the faulting process: if the object gets turned into a fault, the value of the transient property will be cleared out. (We'll talk about faulting in depth in the chapter about accessing data.)

Before we implement our custom getter and setter for the transient colors property, we first have to talk about primitive properties. Each **@NSManaged** property on a managed object subclass has an underlying *primitive* property with accessor methods that are generated dynamically by Core Data. The primitive accessor methods give you access to the managed object's internal storage. To satisfy the compiler, we have to declare the primitive property like this:

@NSManaged private var primitiveColors: [UIColor]?

Like colorStorage, primitiveColors is also declared as private because it's an implementation detail. Now we're ready to implement the custom setter and getter for the colors property, where we can leverage the same functions we used above to perform the transformation between NSData and [UIColor]:

```
public private(set) var colors: [UIColor] {
    get {
        willAccessValueForKey(Keys.Colors)
        var c = primitiveColors
        didAccessValueForKey(Keys.Colors)
        if c == nil {
            c = colorStorage.moodColors ?? []
            primitiveColors = c
        }
        return c!
    }
    set {
        willChangeValueForKey(Keys.Colors)
        primitiveColors = newValue
        didChangeValueForKey(Keys.Colors)
        colorStorage = newValue.moodData
    }
}
```

The important bit of this code is that we wrap access to the primitiveColors property with willAccessValueForKey(_:) and didAccessValueForKey(_:) calls in the getter, and with willChangeValueForKey(_:) and didChangeValueForKey(_:) calls in the setter. This allows Core Data to perform its usual housekeeping behind the scenes.

> Here we use custom overloads of the willAccess/didAccess and willChange/didChange methods that accept an argument of type RawRepresentable backed by String. This way, we can define the keys in a string-backed enum and get autocompletion when using them. See the code on GitHub for more details.

The custom getter will only perform the transformation from binary data to an array of colors the first time you access this property. The setter, on the other hand, will perform the transformation from an array of colors to binary data each time you set a new value on the colors property. If that's too expensive, there's an alternative approach: you can move the transformation step from the setter to the managed object's willSave() method to only perform this step one time per save. This approach is also described in the Core Data Programming Guide.

A similar though more lightweight use case for custom accessors is when you want to store an enum value in Core Data. Let's say we have the following managed object subclass with an enum **Type** that we want to persist:

```
class Message: ManagedObject {
    enum Type: Int16 {
        case Text = 1
        case Image = 2
    }
    // ...
}
```

The approach is the same as before. We declare the primitive version of the property as private and then implement the public-facing property with the correct type:

```
class Message: ManagedObject {
    @NSManaged private var primitiveType: NSNumber

    static let typeKey = "type"
    var type: Type {
```

```
    get {
        willAccessValueForKey(Message.typeKey)
        guard let val = Type(rawValue: primitiveType.shortValue)
            else { fatalError("invalid enum value") }
        didAccessValueForKey(Message.typeKey)
        return val
    }
    set {
        willChangeValueForKey(Message.typeKey)
        primitiveType = NSNumber(short: newValue.rawValue)
        didChangeValueForKey(Message.typeKey)
    }
  }
 }
}
```

Another use case for a custom setter on Core Data properties is to update other (internal) properties when setting a new value. In the text chapter, we show an example of this: setting a string property automatically updates another internal property with a normalized form of this string.

Default Values and Optional Values

Attributes of all data types can have a default value. Core Data will automatically set this value on the attribute as an object is inserted into its context. This can be very useful to ensure objects start out with sane values, but it is even more useful in combination with non-optional values in Swift. You can set the default values in Xcode's model editor.

By default, all attributes on Core Data managed objects are optional: they can either have a value or be **nil**. You can, though, make a Core Data attribute non-optional and use a non-optional type for the corresponding property in your managed object subclass. Ensuring that values are non-**nil** is particularly important when working with predicates. **nil** has special meaning in these cases. The chapter on predicates goes into more details about this.

You can also set default values at runtime. A good example of this is the date attribute on our *Mood* entity. Whenever we create a new mood, we want to set the current date and time. To do that, we overwrite awakeFromInsert() in the Mood class:

```
public final class Mood: ManagedObject {
    // ...
```

```
public override func awakeFromInsert() {
    super.awakeFromInsert()
    primitiveDate = NSDate()
}
@NSManaged private var primitiveDate: NSDate
// ...
}
```

awakeFromInsert() is only invoked once in an object's lifetime, namely when the object is first created. After having called the superclass's implementation, we initialize the date. You might have noticed that we're using the primitive variant of the date property again. The reason for this is that we don't want this change to be tracked as a change in the managed object; we simply want it to be the default state of the object.

Summary

In this chapter, we explored Core Data's default data types and possibilities for storing other custom data types. For custom types, you always need to convert your custom data to one of the supported basic types in order to persist the data. To achieve this, you can just let your type conform to NSCoding and use a transformable attribute, you can specify your own value transformer, or you can implement custom accessor methods.

Which approach you should take depends a lot on your use case. Don't make it more complicated than it has to be, and do some real profiling to verify any worries about performance you might have.

Takeaways

→ Core Data supports a wide range of basic types out of the box. Choose the one that fits your use case without unnecessarily wasting space.

→ When storing binary data, always enable the option to allow external storage, especially if the binary data is large.

→ The easiest way to persist custom data types is to simply make them conform to NSCoding. Use this option if you don't have valid concerns about storage size or performance.

→ If you need to implement a more efficient storage format, consider whether or not the transformation should happen lazily. If so, implement your custom accessor methods. Otherwise, you can provide a custom value transformer.

→ When implementing custom accessors, always remember to wrap access to primitive properties in willAccess.../didAccess... or willChange.../didChange... calls.

→ Mark attributes as non-optional by default and only make exceptions if you have to. This applies especially to numeric attributes.

→ Next to the static default values you can specify in the model editor, you can set default values at runtime by overriding awakeFromInsert().

Part 2
Understanding
Core Data

Accessing Data

In this chapter, we will dive into the details of how all the parts of Core Data play together when you access persisted data in various ways. We will also take a look at the advanced options Core Data exposes to gain more control over the whole process. Later on, we'll discuss one of the major reasons for all this machinery under the hood: memory efficiency and performance. Core Data does a lot of heavy lifting in order for you to be able to work with huge datasets.

You don't need to know all this to use Core Data in straightforward scenarios. However, it can be helpful to have an understanding of what's happening behind the scenes once you're dealing with more complex setups or large-scale setups with thousands of objects.

Throughout this chapter, we'll assume that we're working with the default SQLite persistent store.

Fetch Requests

Fetch requests are the most obvious way to get objects from Core Data. Let's take a look at what happens when you execute a very simple fetch request without touching any of its configuration options:

```
let request = NSFetchRequest(entityName: "Mood")
let moods = try! moc.executeFetchRequest(request)
```

Let's go through this step by step:

1. The context forwards the fetch request to its persistent store coordinator by calling executeRequest(_:withContext:). Note how the context passes itself on as the second argument — this will be used later on.

2. The persistent store coordinator forwards the request to all of its persistent stores (in case you have multiple) by calling each store's executeRequest(_:withContext:) method. Again: the context from which the fetch request originated is passed to the store.

3. The persistent store converts the fetch request into an SQL statement and sends this query to SQLite.

4. SQLite executes the query on the data in the store's database file(s) and returns all rows matching this query to the store (cf. the chapter about SQLite for more on this). The rows contain both the object IDs and the raw data (since the fetch request's includesPropertyValues option is **true**

by default). Object IDs uniquely identify records in the store — in fact, they are a combination of the store's ID, the table's ID, and the row's primary key in the table.

The raw data that's returned is comprised of simple data types: numbers, strings, and binary blobs. It is stored in the persistent store's *row cache* associated with the object IDs and with a timestamp of when the cache entry was last updated. A row cache entry with a certain object ID lives as long as a managed object with this object ID exists, whether it is a fault or not.

5. The persistent store instantiates managed objects for the object IDs it received from the SQLite store and returns them to the coordinator. It's crucial for the store to be able to call objectWithID(_:) on the originating context for this, because managed objects are tied to one specific context.

   The default behavior of fetch requests is to return managed objects (there are other result types, but we'll set them aside for a bit). Those objects are *faults* by default, i.e. they are lightweight objects that are not populated with the actual data yet. They are promises to get the data once you need it (more on faulting below).

   However, if an object with the same object ID already exists in the context, then this existing object will be used unchanged. This is called *uniquing*: Core Data guarantees that within a managed object context, there's only a single object representing a certain piece of data, no matter how you get to it. Put differently: objects representing the same data within the same managed object context will compare equal using pointer equality.

6. The persistent store coordinator returns to the context the array of managed objects it got from the persistent store.

7. Before returning the results of the fetch request, the context considers its pending changes and updates the results accordingly, since the includesPendingChanges flag on the fetch request is **true** by default. (Pending changes are any updates, inserts, and deletions you've made within the managed object context that haven't yet been saved.) Additional objects may be added to the result, or objects may be removed because they no longer match.

8. Finally, an array with managed objects matching the fetch request is returned to the caller.

All of this happens synchronously — the managed object context and the persistent store coordinator are blocked until the fetch request is finished:

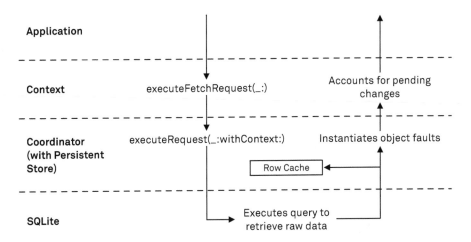

Figure 4.1: A fetch request makes a round trip all the way down to the SQLite store

At this point, you have an array of managed objects representing the data you asked for in the fetch request. However, since these objects are faults, a few more things have to happen to actually access the data of these objects. We'll look at them in the next section.

The most important parts in this process are Core Data's *faulting* and *uniquing* mechanisms. Faulting allows you to work with large datasets without materializing all objects in memory. Uniquing makes sure that you always get the same object for the same piece of data, and that there's only a single copy of this object.

Object Faults

You can control whether a fetch request returns faults or fully materialized objects via the returnsObjectsAsFaults property, which is **true** by default. Set it to **false** in order to force Core Data to pre-populate the returned objects with the actual data. This makes sense if you know up front that you'll need all the data anyway. In such a case, you can save a bunch of round trips to the persistent store layer to fulfill the faults. This is a small performance gain, even if the data is in the row cache.

When an object is a fault and you access one of its properties, the following steps are triggered to retrieve the data:

1. Core Data's property accessor calls willAccessValueForKey(_:) internally, and this method checks if the object is a fault.

   Core Data implements the property accessor methods for **@NSManaged** properties at runtime, and therefore can inject its own behavior into reading and writing property values, like fulfilling a fault. That's also how Core Data notices when you make a change to a property. This is done so that the object is tracked as having pending changes and needing to be saved.

2. Because the object is a fault, it will tell its context to fulfill the fault, i.e. to retrieve the missing data. The context, in turn, asks its persistent store coordinator for that data.

3. The persistent store coordinator asks the persistent store for the data associated with the object's ID by calling the newValuesForObjectWithID(_:withContext:) method.

4. The persistent store looks up the data for this object ID in its row cache. If the cached data is not yet stale, we have a cache hit, the data is returned, and we're done.

   Staleness of the cached data is determined by the context's stalenessInterval property. By default, it's set to 0, which means that the cached data never gets stale, and the persistent store coordinator always returns cached data if it's present. If you set the stalenessInterval to a positive value, the cached data is only used if its last update is no longer ago than the staleness interval indicates in seconds.

5. If we had a cache miss or the cached data was out of date, the persistent store generates the appropriate SQL statement to retrieve the data from SQLite. It then executes it and returns the data to the coordinator. The newly fetched data also gets stored in the row cache.

6. The coordinator now returns the data to the context, and the managed object gets populated with this data: it turns from a fault to a materialized object, or, in Core Data parlance, the fault has been fulfilled.

   In this step, the raw data from the row cache gets copied and transformed into the correct data types for the managed object. For example, transformable attributes will be converted from their NSData representations to what their user-facing types are. Furthermore, the

context will keep a snapshot of this data for the purpose of conflict
detection and resolution when you save changes to the object later on.
You can read more on this in the next chapter about changing and
saving data.

7. Finally, the property value you accessed on the managed object is
   returned:

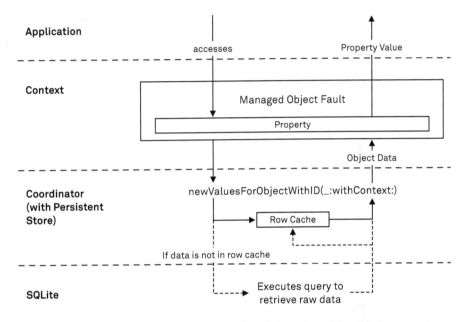

Figure 4.2: Fulfilling an object fault fetches the data from SQLite if it's not already in the row cache

As you can see, fulfilling a fault from the row cache is a relatively cheap
operation — everything's happening in memory. However, if the data is not
present in the row cache, or if it is stale, fulfilling a fault triggers a round trip to
the database to get the latest values.

After executing a normal fetch request (i.e. where returnsObjectsAsFaults and
includesPropertyValues both are **true**), the row cache will be populated with all
the data you asked for. As a result, fulfilling the returned faults is rather cheap
— it's a tradeoff of higher memory usage for the ability to fulfill any of the
returned faults very quickly.

However, by setting includesPropertyValues to **false**, you can change this
default behavior for a particular fetch request and prevent it from loading any

of the attribute values — except the object IDs — from the database. Fetching only object IDs can be very useful in and of itself. For example, Core Data's mechanism to fetch results in batches takes advantage of this. We'll look at this particular example in more detail below.

Fulfilling a fault for an object that has been fetched with includesPropertyValues set to **false** causes another round trip to SQLite, unless the data has already been retrieved in another way. The up-front cost of such a fetch request is low, but using the objects can be expensive.

We'll talk more about the performance characteristics of the different layers of the Core Data stack in the performance chapter.

Refreshing Objects

Of course, you can also go the other way and turn a materialized managed object into a fault. To do that, call the context's refreshObject(_:mergeChanges:) method for individual objects. The second argument, mergeChanges, only matters if the object has unsaved changes. In this case, a **true** value will not turn the object into a fault; instead, it will update the unchanged properties from the row cache, preserving any unsaved changes. That's almost always what you want to do (and what refreshAllObjects() does as well).

If you specify **false** for mergeChanges, the object will be forced to turn into a fault, and unsaved changes will be lost. Use this with great caution, especially with regard to pending changes in relationships. In this case, forcing an object to turn into a fault could introduce referential integrity issues into your data. This is because one direction of a bi-directional relationship might have been compromised by the refresh.

Fetch requests have the option of shouldRefreshRefetchedObjects, which will cause the context to automatically refresh all existing objects in the context that are also part of the fetch result. By default, an existing materialized object will not be changed by a fetch request. Setting shouldRefreshRefetchedObjects to **true** is a convenient way to make sure the returned objects have the latest values from the persistent store.[1]

---

1 At the time of writing, shouldRefreshRefetchedObjects is not working. The problem is tracked as radar rdar://21855854.

Fetch Request Result Types

Normally, when you execute a fetch request, you'll get back an array of managed objects. However, there are other result types you can request by changing the resultType property on the fetch request. Next to the default, there are three other options: fetching only object IDs, fetching specific properties as dictionaries, and fetching only the count of the matching rows.

Fetching only the IDs of the objects is straightforward: just set the result type to .ManagedObjectIDResultType, and the fetch request will return an array of NSManagedObjectID instances instead of the usual managed objects. But note that such a fetch request will still load all data for the matching rows from the database, updating the coordinator's row cache. If you want to prevent that, you have to also set includesPropertyValues to **false** on the fetch request.

Fetching only object IDs can be very useful. For example, we can set up a fetch request with the predicate and sort descriptors as desired, but specify the object ID result type and set includesPropertyValues to **false**. This will return a fixed list of object IDs at very little cost. We can iterate over this list, fetching the data incrementally by passing the required object IDs into a **self** IN %@ predicate. This is, in fact, how Core Data implements a fetch batch size on a fetch request.

The result type, .CountResultType, is conceptually identical to using countForFetchRequest(_:) instead of executeFetchRequest(_:). Whenever you only need to know the number of results, make sure to use this instead of executing a regular fetch request and counting the results.

Lastly, there's .DictionaryResultType. This one is a bit more complicated, but it's very powerful. The basic idea is this: instead of returning an array of managed objects that represent the data you asked for, a fetch request with a dictionary result type will return an array of dictionaries containing the raw data. This enables a few interesting use cases.

To start with, you can specify to only retrieve certain attributes of an entity by setting propertiesToFetch. Core Data will then only load those particular attributes into memory, which can be a win in terms of performance and memory footprint if you're operating on a very large table.

However, the more interesting part is that this kind of fetch request allows us to harness more of the power of SQLite to do all kinds of operations on our data. Let's say we have an *Employee* entity that has a type attribute and a salary attribute. We want to know the average salary of the employees, grouped by the type of employee. Instead of fetching all employee objects, looping over them, and aggregating those values manually, we can use the dictionary result type to do this in a much more performant and memory-efficient way:

```
let request = NSFetchRequest(entityName: "Employee")
request.resultType = .DictionaryResultType

let salaryExp = NSExpressionDescription()
salaryExp.expressionResultType = .DoubleAttributeType
salaryExp.expression = NSExpression(forFunction: "average:",
    arguments: [NSExpression(forKeyPath: "salary")])
salaryExp.name = "avgSalary"

request.propertiesToGroupBy = ["type"]
request.propertiesToFetch = ["type", salaryExp]

try! context.executeFetchRequest(request)
```

We're using two properties on NSFetchRequest that are only applicable when using the dictionary result type: propertiesToGroupBy and propertiesToFetch. In propertiesToGroupBy, we specify the name of the attribute that should be used to group the data before the SELECT statement is executed (if you're unfamiliar with SQL, check out the chapter on SQLite). In propertiesToFetch, we specify which attributes should be retrieved. These don't have to be existing attributes — in our case, we use an NSExpression object to create a computed attribute that aggregates the salaries by averaging them.

The result of this fetch request will be an array of dictionaries with two keys: "type" and "avgSalary" (the name of the salaryExp). NSExpression has many supported functions you can use to compose calculated values; check out the class documentation for more details. If you need to do calculations on large datasets, you can get things done in a vastly more efficient way using this approach.

Fetching in Batches

There's another property on NSFetchRequest that alters the steps we've discussed above quite considerably: fetchBatchSize. It's very simple to use, but under the hood, Core Data goes to great lengths to enable this feature.

Imagine you have stored 100,000 objects of one type in your database, and you want to show them in a table view. If you would use a standard fetch request like we've done above, Core Data would return an array of 100,000 faults — a lot of objects to be instantiated. However, Core Data will also load all the raw data for 100,000 rows from SQLite into the row cache, which is a huge overhead that is, in all likelihood, unnecessary.

Here's where fetchBatchSize comes in. For example, we configure the fetch request for the mood table view like this:

```
let request = Mood.sortedFetchRequestWithPredicate(moodSource.predicate)
request.returnsObjectsAsFaults = false
request.fetchBatchSize = 20
```

When we execute this fetch request, the following steps occur:

1. The persistent store loads all the primary keys (the object IDs) into memory and hands them back to the coordinator. In this step, predicates and sort descriptors are still applied, but the result of this query is only a list of object IDs, instead of all the data associated with them.

2. The persistent store coordinator builds a special kind of array that is backed by the object IDs and returns the array to the context. Note that this array is not an array of faults, as we've seen above. Its count and the positions of the elements in it are fixed due to the object ID backing. But the array is not populated by any data — it's a promise to get the data when necessary.

Once you access an element of the array, Core Data will do the heavy lifting under the hood to pull in the data in pages. This occurs as follows:

1. The batched array notices that it's lacking the data for the element you're trying to access, and it will ask the context to load a batch of fetchBatchSize objects around the index you've asked for.

2. As usual, this request gets forwarded through the persistent store coordinator to the persistent store, where an appropriate SQL statement is executed to load the data for this batch from SQLite. The raw data is stored in the row cache, and the managed objects are returned to the coordinator.

3. Since we've set returnsObjectsAsFaults to **false**, the coordinator asks the store for the full data, populates the objects with it, and returns them to the context.

4. The batch array returns the object you've asked for and keeps the other objects in this batch around in case you need one of them next.

As we loop through the array, Core Data will pull in additional batches of objects as needed and keep a small number of these batches around on a least recently used basis. Old batches will get released. Thus, using fetchBatchSize allows us to iterate through incredibly large sets of objects in an extremely memory-efficient way.

It is worth noting that it often makes sense to combine the use of a fetch batch size with setting returnsObjectsAsFaults to **false**. This is because we're only pulling in the data for a small batch of objects at a time. Additionally, it's likely that we'll need the data for this batch immediately — for example, for populating a table or collection view.

Asynchronous Fetch Requests

The API we have used to execute fetch requests thus far has been synchronous, i.e. the call will block until the results are returned. However, there's another API available for executing a fetch request asynchronously. This way, the call will return immediately, and your program will continue to run while Core Data fetches the data in the background. It then calls you back once the results are in:

```
let fetchRequest = NSFetchRequest(entityName: "Mood")
let asyncRequest = NSAsynchronousFetchRequest(fetchRequest: fetchRequest) {
    result in
    if let result = result.finalResult {
        // Results are in!
    }
}
try! context.executeRequest(asyncRequest)
```

You can use all the features of normal fetch requests on asynchronous fetch requests as well. Asynchronous fetch requests also integrate with the NSProgress API, which you can use to monitor progress or even cancel ongoing requests. This can be helpful if you need to kick off expensive fetch requests on large datasets. An example of this is searching with non-trivial predicates, where the results might not be needed anymore by the time they come in.

Relationships

Fetch requests are not the only mechanism to retrieve managed objects. In fact, fetch requests should often be avoided, as we will argue for in more detail in the performance chapter. An alternative is to traverse a relationship property to get to the desired objects.

We've already talked in detail about object faults and what happens to fulfill them. When it comes to accessing relationships, there's a similar concept involved: *relationship faults*.

The fact that relationships on a managed object can be faults — even if the object itself is fully materialized — is a powerful feature. It allows you to load objects into memory without automatically pulling in the whole object graph that might be associated with those objects. Only when you traverse a relationship do more and more parts of the object graph get pulled into memory.

Relationship faults function differently for to-one and to-many relationships. Let's look at the simpler to-one case first. For example, consider the continent relationship on the *Country* entity from our example app. If you have a country object (that itself is not a fault) and access the continent property, Core Data uses the object ID stored in the to-one relationship to instantiate the associated Continent object. If this continent object hasn't been loaded into the context before, it will be a fault at this point. Once you access any of its properties, this fault will be fulfilled, as we described above already.

The other side of this relationship, countries on Continent, is more complicated since it is a to-many relationship. To-many relationship faults are two-level faults. When you access the continent's countries relationship, Core Data will fulfill the first level by asking the database for the object IDs of the related country objects. At this point, no data for the country objects has been loaded yet — the returned country objects are all faults with data that is not in the row cache yet (assuming it wasn't already there for some unrelated reason). Only when we access a property on one of those country faults will Core Data get the data and populate the fault for this specific object.

While relationship faults are a powerful feature to keep the memory footprint small when working on large datasets, there are scenarios where repeatedly fulfilling faults from the database can become a performance issue. We'll discuss ways to alleviate this potential issue in the section about fetch requests in the performance chapter.

Other Ways to Retrieve Managed Objects

Next to executing fetch requests and traversing relationships, there are a few other ways to get to managed objects.

Each managed object context holds a list of all objects currently registered with it in the registeredObjects property. To retrieve an object with a specific ID, you can call objectRegisteredForID(_:) on the context. This returns **nil** if no object with the specified ID is known to the context. However, this doesn't mean that no such object exists in the persistent store. objectRegisteredForID(_:) never performs any I/O; it simply consults the context's registeredObjects.

You can also use objectWithID(_:) on the managed object context. If an object is already registered with the given ID, this method will return that object. But if no such object is registered with the context, the context will create a managed object that is a fault and has the given object ID.

This method will not do any checks to make sure such an object exists. It's very naive — it assumes you know what you are doing. If you specify a non-existing ID, you will get back a fault with this ID, but you will crash as soon as you try to access any of its properties. However, because this method doesn't do any checking, it is extremely fast.

Lastly, there's existingObjectWithID(_:). Just like the two previous methods, if an object with the given ID is already registered with the context, it simply returns that object. If not, it will try to fetch the given object from the persistent store. If no object with this ID exists in the store, the method throws an error. Because of this, existingObjectWithID(_:) can potentially be slow, as it has to perform a round trip to the database in order to get the data for the specified object ID.

Memory Considerations

Much of what we discussed above has the purpose of managing memory efficiently. Core Data goes to great lengths to make it possible to work with huge datasets, pulling in only the parts of the object graph currently needed. The fact that objects (and their relationships) are returned as faults by default, and that we can fetch data in sensible batches, makes it relatively easy to deal with large amounts of data while maintaining a small memory footprint.

Faulting is not only useful to keep the memory footprint small during normal operation; it's also a good tool to respond to memory warnings your app may receive on iOS. You can simply re-fault all objects that don't have pending changes by calling refreshAllObjects() on your managed object contexts, thereby freeing memory you don't need at a given moment.

Managed Objects and Their Contexts

By default, the managed object context only keeps a strong reference to managed objects that have pending changes. This means that objects your code doesn't have a strong reference to will be removed from the context's registeredObjects set and be deallocated. The same thing also applies to the data the persistent store holds in its row cache: as soon as no managed object references this data anymore (i.e. no managed object exists with an object ID that matches an entry in the row cache), the data will be evicted from the row cache.

This default behavior helps to keep only the part of the object graph that you're currently working with in memory, be it as fully realized managed objects, or as raw data waiting to be used in the row cache. However, there are scenarios where you'd want to keep more than that in memory, because you know you will need a certain set of objects over and over. In these cases, you should simply keep the desired objects around by, for example, storing them in an array you keep a strong reference to. (The context has a retainsRegisteredObjects property to make it keep strong references to all its registered objects, but its usage is discouraged by Apple, since it can easily lead to very high memory use.)

There's one more pitfall related to the issue of retaining objects: a managed object context can have an undo manager associated with it. On OS X, this is on by default. The undo manager will hold on to all objects you've ever modified in this context in order to be able to undo anything that's been done. This will undermine the mechanism described above, which strives to only keep what's needed in memory. If you don't need undo management, be sure to disable this behavior by setting the undoManager property to **nil**.

Relationship Reference Cycles

Once relationships come into play, managed objects can have references to other managed objects. An object and its data may therefore be kept alive by the context simply because it is referenced by another object. And because relationships are bidirectional, once a relationship has been traversed in both directions, we'll end up with a reference cycle:

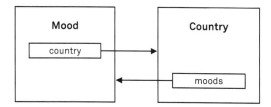

Figure 4.3: Accessing a relationship from both sides creates a reference cycle between the two objects

To break such a cycle, we have to refresh at least one of the involved objects. Using the context's refreshObject(_:mergeChanges:) method, the object will remain valid, but its data will be gone from the context. This not only affects the object's properties, but also its relationships, thus breaking any existing reference cycles the object is a part of:

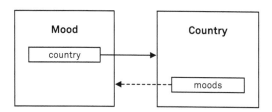

Figure 4.4: Relationship reference cycles can be broken by refreshing at least one of the objects

The point at which it's best to break relationship reference cycles depends on your use case. One possibility is to refresh objects when you don't need them anymore — for example, when popping a view controller off the stack. Another possibility is to refresh all objects when your app enters the background.

On this note, it's worthwhile to mention that refreshing an object that's actively used by your app (and which therefore has to be materialized again) is not as bad as it sounds. As long as you hold a strong reference to it, its data will remain in the row cache, and fulfilling the fault will not be very expensive.

As always, the profiling and debugging tools discussed in a later chapter are your friends to find the right tradeoff between memory footprint and performance.

Summary

In order to be able to work on large datasets in a memory-efficient way, Core Data does a lot of heavy lifting for us. It does this by only keeping the part of the object graph that we currently need in memory. The key parts to make this possible are object and relationship faults, as well as batched fetch requests.

To achieve this, Core Data has a multilayered architecture, where each level has different performance and memory tradeoffs. Objects registered in the managed object context are fastest to work with but have the highest memory impact. Fulfilling object faults from the persistent store's row cache is a bit more expensive, but in return, the row cache stores the data in a more memory-efficient way. Fetch requests always retrieve their data from the underlying SQLite database and are therefore expensive in comparison, but they guarantee to always return the latest persisted data.

If we have to do calculations on large datasets, we can use the dictionary result type to harness the power of SQLite to efficiently apply aggregate functions without ever pulling those objects into memory.

Takeaways

→ Fetch requests always take a round trip to the database, pull the data into the row cache, and return object faults by default.

→ Faults are lightweight objects that are not yet populated with data. Accessing a property on a fault causes it to retrieve its data, which is called *fulfilling*.

→ Fulfilling an object fault can be relatively cheap if the data is in the row cache. Otherwise, it will be fetched from the database. This can become expensive if many of the round trips are performed for individual objects.

→ Fetch requests have various options that expose a great amount of control over what they actually do, including whether the results should be returned as faults, whether the actual attribute data should be loaded at all, etc.

→ Use the fetchBatchSize property to avoid pulling in data for all rows at once. If you're not absolutely sure that you will need all results right away, you should use this property.

→ Be aware that accessing a relationship between two objects from both sides leads to a reference cycle. You should break the cycle by refreshing at least one object in the cycle at an appropriate time.

Changing and Saving Data

In this chapter, we'll take an in-depth look at what happens in the Core Data stack when you make changes to the data — from change tracking over conflict detection to persisting the data. Furthermore, we will look at the more advanced APIs for making changes to many objects at once and explore how they work and what you have to do to use them successfully.

As in the previous chapter, we'll assume that we're working with the default SQLite persistent store.

Change Tracking

Each managed object context keeps track of all the changes you make to managed objects that belong to it. But before we go into the details, we first have to look at the big picture of change tracking. Change tracking happens on two different levels:

1. Between calls to save()

   In order to persist the changes you've made in a certain context, Core Data needs to know which objects have been inserted, deleted, and updated. Core Data even keeps track of which specific attributes on each unsaved object have changed. This fine-grained change tracking is important for resolving conflicts, but we'll talk more about this later. Saving a context triggers an NSManagedObjectContextDidSaveNotification, which contains information about all the changes made since the last save.

2. Between calls to processPendingChanges()

   This method usually gets called multiple times between saves — for example, it is invoked after each closure passed to performBlock(_:) has run. Processing pending changes triggers an NSManagedObjectContextObjectsDidChangeNotification, which contains information about all the changes made since the last notification of this kind.

Let's first look in more detail at the second kind of change tracking: the objects-did-change notification loop.

Usually you don't need to call processPendingChanges() yourself. Core Data will invoke this method automatically (e.g. before changes get saved and at the end of a call to performBlock(_:)). When it's called, the following things happen:

1. Deletes are propagated across relationships according to their delete rules.

   You can change this default behavior by setting propagatesDeletesAtEndOfEvent on the context to **false**, so that deletes will only be propagated during saves.

2. Insertions and deletions in relationships are propagated to the corresponding inverse relationships.

3. The pending changes are coalesced and registered as an undo action (if the context has an undo manager).

4. The context posts an NSManagedObjectContextObjectsDidChangeNotification.

   This notification's userInfo dictionary contains the sets of objects that have been inserted, updated, deleted, and refreshed since the last time processPendingChanges() was called.

When you listen to the objects-did-change notification, you can get even more fine-tuned information about what has changed since the last objects-did-change notification was posted. Calling changedValuesForCurrentEvent() on a changed object returns a dictionary with entries containing information about changes on the property level: the dictionary's keys are the names of the changed properties, while the dictionary's values are the *old* values of those properties.

Listening to the objects-did-change notification and evaluating changedValuesForCurrentEvent() is a useful reactive approach to updating the UI when an object changes. It's used, for example, by NSFetchedResultsController, but we've also already used it ourselves to build a managed object observer that notifies us when an object gets deleted.

Next up, let's take a look at Core Data's change tracking between saves.

You can ask managed objects and their contexts for unsaved changes. On managed objects, the following APIs are available:

→ hasChanges — a simple "dirty" flag indicating that this object needs to be saved. (This flag is the combination of the following three properties.)

→ inserted — indicating that this object has been newly created and has never been saved before.

→ deleted — indicating that this object has been deleted and will be removed from the database with the next save.

→ updated — indicating that this object has been changed, i.e. if you have invoked any setters on Core Data properties.

If you want to find out if the values of a managed object have actually changed when compared to the persisted data, you should use hasPersistentChangedValues. This flag compares the current values to the last known persisted state of the object and only reports it to be changed if the values are actually different. Note that the comparison is not performed against the data in the store, but instead against the data that was last saved to or fetched from the store.

Next to finding out *if* something has changed on a managed object, you can also check *what* has changed. Calling changedValues() returns a dictionary with the changed keys and *new* values since the object was last saved or fetched. In case you want to know the old values of any property (and not just the ones that have been changed), you can call committedValuesForKeys(_:). To get all old values, simply pass in **nil**.

So far, we've only discussed how to check for changes since the last save on individual managed objects. However, you can also ask the managed object context itself if it has unsaved changes by using the following properties on the context:

→ hasChanges is a simple "dirty" flag that is **true** if the context has any pending changes that need to be saved.

→ insertedObjects, updatedObjects, and deletedObjects are sets of objects whose inserted, updated, and deleted flags are **true**, respectively.

Now that we've discussed how Core Data keeps track of unsaved changes, we will go into more detail about what happens when you actually save those changes.

Saving Changes

Once you've made changes within a managed object context, you want to persist those changes at some point. In this section, we're going to look at how the saving process works and how conflicts are dealt with.

Core Data saves changes *transactionally,* i.e. a set of pending changes either succeeds to be saved as a whole, or none of those changes gets persisted. If the save fails, you have several options to deal with this situation, but we'll look at those later.

When you call save() on a context, the following things happen:

1. processPendingChanges() gets called and posts an objects-did-change notification as described above.

2. An NSManagedObjectContextWillSaveNotification gets posted.

3. Validation is run on all changed objects.

   If validation fails, the save process is aborted and an error of type NSManagedObjectValidationError or NSValidationMultipleErrorsError is thrown. Validation rules can be set up in the data model editor as well as in code. See the section below for more details.

4. willSave() gets called on all managed objects with unsaved changes.

   You can override this method in your NSManagedObject subclasses and use it to e.g. lazily serialize custom data types. If you make further changes to managed objects at this point (or have made changes during the previous validation step), Core Data will keep cycling through the sequence of processPendingChanges(), followed by validation, and then calling of willSave() on all unsaved objects, until a stable state is reached.

   It's your responsibility to not create an infinite loop here. For example, if you make changes in willSave(), you should test for equality before you invoke the setter, since setting a property is recognized as a change, even if the value stays the same.

5. An NSSaveChangesRequest is created and sent to the persistent store coordinator. This save request contains four sets of objects: inserted, updated, deleted, and locked.

   The locked objects set contains objects that have not been changed but that should nevertheless participate in the conflict detection process. In the meantime, if any of those objects have changed in the persistent store, the save will fail. You can mark unchanged objects to participate in conflict detection by calling detectConflictsForObject(_:) on the context.

6. The persistent store coordinator obtains permanent object IDs from the store for the newly inserted objects by calling its obtainPermanentIDsForObjects(_:) method.

   This is necessary, since only the persistent store has final authority over the primary keys in its tables. When you insert a new object, the context uses a temporary ID, which will be replaced during the save request. (You can check if an ID is temporary using NSManagedObjectID's temporaryID flag.)

   When we look at Core Data's SQL debug output in the profiling chapter, you can see this happening as a separate transaction in SQLite before the actual save happens.

7. The persistent store coordinator forwards the request to the persistent store.

8. The persistent store checks whether or not the data of the objects you're trying to save has changed in the row cache since the context you're saving last fetched this data.

   Core Data maintains so-called snapshots of the raw data for each managed object. These snapshots represent the last known state of the data in the persistent store. During the save, these snapshots can be compared to the data in the row cache: if the data in the row cache has changed, the save fails or proceeds depending on the context's merge policy. We'll look at the conflict case later, but for now, let's assume there are no conflicts and the save proceeds normally.

9. The save request is translated into an SQL query, which updates the data in the SQLite database.

   This is another potential point of conflict. The data in the SQLite database might have changed since the data in the object to be saved was fetched. How Core Data handles this also depends on the context's merge policy. For now, let's assume again that no conflict occurs.

10. After a successful save, the persistent store's row cache gets updated with the new values.

11. didSave() gets called on all managed objects that have been saved.

12. Finally, an NSManagedObjectContextDidSaveNotification is posted.

This notification's userInfo dictionary contains sets with the objects that have been inserted, updated, and deleted. One primary use case of this notification is to merge the saved changes into another managed object context by passing it to its mergeChangesFromContextDidSaveNotification(_:) method. We'll see more of this in the chapter about syncing and concurrency.

Validation

As outlined above, each time Core Data attempts to save pending changes, it first checks the validity of the changed data according to the rules you've provided.

You can set up simple validation rules, such as minimum and maximum values of an integer attribute, in Xcode's Data Model Editor. However, you can also specify more complex rules in code.

Validation works on two levels: on the property level, and on the object level. For property-level validation, you can implement individual methods for each property within your managed object subclass. These methods have to follow the naming scheme validate<PropertyName> — for example:

```
public func validateLongitude(
    value: AutoreleasingUnsafeMutablePointer<AnyObject?>) throws
{
    guard let l = (value.memory as? NSNumber)?.doubleValue else { return }
    if l < -180 || l > 180 {
        throw propertyValidationErrorForKey("longitude",
            localizedDescription: "longitude has to be in range -180...180")
    }
}
```

First, we get the value out of the unsafe mutable pointer passed to this method and cast it to the type of the property we're validating. We do this within a guard statement so that we simply return in case the value is nil (since this particular property is optional). Then we do whatever checks are required and throw an instance of NSError with error code NSManagedObjectValidationError if those checks fail. We use an extension on NSManagedObject, propertyValidationErrorForKey(_:localizedDescription:), to construct such error instances. See the code on GitHub[1] for the details.

Instead of throwing an error, you can also fix the invalid value if it makes sense in your use case. In the example above, we could have decided to let the longitude value wrap around so that it's always between -180 and 180:

```
public func validateLongitude(
    value: AutoreleasingUnsafeMutablePointer<AnyObject?>) throws
{
    guard let l = (value.memory as? NSNumber)?.doubleValue else { return }
    if abs(l) > 180 {
        value.memory = -l/abs(l) * 180 + l % 180
    }
}
```

You have to be careful with touching the setters of Core Data properties from within validation code. Validation code will be run repeatedly until a stable state is reached (i.e. no new changes have been introduced). If you always dirty a managed object during validation, you'll be stuck in an infinite loop.

Next to property-level validation, you can also implement validation rules that operate across properties. For this purpose, you overwrite validateForInsert(), validateForUpdate(), or validateForDelete(). You should call **super** in your implementations of these methods. Otherwise, the property-level validation will not take place.

If you want to return multiple validation errors from these methods, you should throw an error with code NSValidationMultipleErrorsError and store the individual errors in the userInfo dictionary under the NSDetailedErrorsKey. It's helpful to wrap all of this in convenience methods so that the code constructing these loosely typed NSError objects is encapsulated in a central place.

If a validation error occurs, the whole save operation will fail — none of the unsaved changes will have been persisted. It's on you to resolve the errors and resave pending changes.

1 https://github.com/objcio/core-data/blob/master/SharedCode/CoreDataErrors.swift

Save Conflicts

When you're working with more than one context simultaneously, conflicts can arise when saving changes. You don't have to worry about this in a simple one-context setup like the one we used in the first part of the book. However, if you're using more complex and potentially concurrent setups, you have to plan ahead for what should happen if such a conflict occurs.

At this point, we'll just give a brief overview of how Core Data does conflict detection. (We'll go into more detail on how to handle those conflicts in the chapter about the complications of complex setups.)

Core Data handles conflicts using a method called optimistic locking. It's referred to as optimistic because checking for conflicts is deferred until the context gets saved.

The gist of it is this: each context maintains snapshots of each managed object's data, which represents the last known persisted state for each object. When you save a context, this snapshot is compared to the data in the row cache, as well as the data in SQLite, to make sure nothing has changed. When something *has* changed, Core Data uses the context's merge policy to resolve the conflict. If you don't specify a merge policy, Core Data's default policy will simply throw an NSManagedObjectMergeError. This error will have detailed information about what went wrong.

Core Data has several predefined merge policies that cover a lot of cases. NSRollbackMergePolicy simply discards changes on objects that caused conflicts. NSOverwriteMergePolicy persists all changes regardless of the conflicts. Additionally, there are two predefined merge policies that operate on the property level: NSMergeByPropertyStoreTrumpMergePolicy and NSMergeByPropertyObjectTrumpMergePolicy merge the data of the changed objects with the persisted data, property by property. With the former, data in the store will prevail in the conflict case. With the latter, in-memory changes will prevail.

For more details on merge policies and how to create custom merge policies, please refer to the chapter about complications of complex setups.

Batch Updates

With iOS 8 and OS X 10.10, Core Data introduced a new API to efficiently do batch updates without having to load all the objects you want to change into memory. One year later, iOS 9 and OS X 10.11 introduced batch deletes that work in a similar way.

While the new batch update and batch delete APIs are welcome additions to the Core Data toolbelt, there's a reason why they didn't exist for a long time: they bypass much of Core Data's normal operating procedures. This may give you a significant performance win in certain situations, but it also means that a lot of things will no longer work in the way you'd otherwise expect them to. In this section, we will go into the details of how batch updates work and what you need to know in order to use them correctly.

The first thing to understand is that batch updates bypass the managed object context and the persistent store coordinator and operate straight on the SQLite database. If you update an attribute or delete a record this way, neither the managed object context nor the coordinator will know of this change. This means that all the usual mechanisms to update the user interface (e.g. NSFetchedResultsController) will not function without you doing extra work. Additionally, you might run into conflicts on subsequent saves if you don't account for changes manually.

Since batch updates operate directly on the SQLite level, even the row cache will be out of date after a batch update if it contained data for all or some of the affected objects. Therefore, it's not enough to refresh managed objects by calling refreshObject(_:mergeChanges:) or even refreshAllObjects() on the context — the objects will be turned into faults, but the row cache still holds the old data. The next time you access a property on one of those objects, the stale data from the row cache will be used again.

This leaves us with two viable options to update the data after batch requests:

1. Use the static mergeChangesFromRemoteContextSave(_:intoContexts:) method on the managed object context class.

   It takes a dictionary as its first argument, which should contain arrays of object IDs under the keys NSInsertedObjectsKey, NSUpdatedObjectsKey, or NSDeletedObjectsKey (depending on the changes you've made). Under the hood, this will also fetch the new data from the store and update the row cache, along with the objects already registered in the context. This API has only been available since iOS 9 / OS X 10.11, but it's our preferred approach.

2. Refetch the data with a fetch request and refresh the objects registered in the context that are part of the fetch request's result set.

    When you use this approach, it makes sense to use the .ManagedObjectIDResultType on the fetch request to avoid unnecessarily creating managed object instances that you don't need. The row cache will still be updated, even if you only ask for the object IDs.

For the first (and preferred) approach, you need all the object IDs for the objects that have been changed by the batch request. We can tell the batch request to return those object IDs by setting its result type to .UpdatedObjectIDsResultType for batch updates or to .ResultTypeObjectIDs for batch deletes. This will return a result of type NSBatchUpdateResult or NSBatchDeleteResult, both of which have a result property that will contain an array of object IDs:

```
batchUpdate.resultType = .UpdatedObjectIDsResultType
guard let result = try! context.executeRequest(batchUpdate) as?
    NSBatchUpdateResult else { fatalError("Wrong result type") }
guard let objectIDs = result.result as? [NSManagedObjectID]
    else { fatalError("Expected object IDs") }
let changes = [NSUpdatedObjectsKey: objectIDs]
NSManagedObjectContext.mergeChangesFromRemoteContextSave(changes,
    intoContexts: [context])
```

Summary

Core Data keeps track of the changes you make on the managed object level and the context level and sends objects-did-change notifications when processPendingChanges() is called. You can use these notifications to react to changes in the data, just as fetched results controllers do. When you save changes, Core Data runs your validation rules and does conflict detection using a two-step optimistic locking approach. It then posts a context-did-save notification if the save succeeded.

Batch updates and deletes are secondary mechanisms to make changes to your data; they bypass all the usual Core Data machinery and go right to the persistent store. This can be very efficient for mass updates (e.g. setting a "read" flag on thousands of objects), but it puts a lot of responsibility on you to make sure that the data in the managed object context and the row cache gets updated accordingly.

Takeaways

→ Core Data tracks changes to managed objects between calls to processPendingChanges(), as well as between calls to save().

→ processPendingChanges() updates relationships and posts the objects-did-change notification, which you can use together with the managed object's changedValuesForCurrentEvent() API to find out what exactly has been changed.

→ Managed objects and managed object contexts have a variety of properties — including but not limited to hasChanges, changedValues(), and insertedObjects — to find out what has changed since the data was last persisted.

→ You can create validation rules on the property and the object level that will be run before changes get saved. The save will fail if any of those rules fail.

→ Saving changes can also fail due to conflicts between the data in the managed object context and the persistent store. Those conflicts can be resolved using appropriate merge policies. However, this only becomes a concern once you're using a setup that is more complex than just a single managed object context.

→ Batch updates and deletes can be powerful tools, but be aware that they work very differently than what you're used to with other Core Data APIs.

Performance

6

In the previous chapters, we talked a lot about how Core Data works internally. In this chapter, we will look at the performance aspects of these internals and how to put this knowledge to use in order to get excellent performance with Core Data.

It is important to note that performance is more than just speed. Tuning your performance makes sure that your app is fast, animations are smooth, and the user doesn't have to wait. But performance is also about energy usage: when you tune your app's performance, you improve battery life. Both energy consumption and speed are affected by the same optimizations. Making sure your app runs well on a slow device will equally benefit users with new and fast devices, as the battery life will be better on those too.

Performance Characteristics of the Core Data Stack

One of the main performance gains comes from understanding the performance characteristics of the Core Data stack and putting them to use:

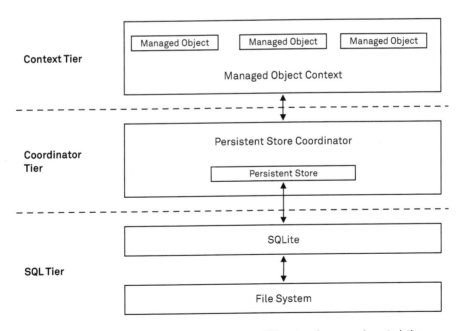

Figure 6.1: The different tiers in the Core Data stack have different performance characteristics

We can roughly divide the Core Data stack into three tiers. As we go down the stack, each tier is exponentially more complex — its performance impact is dramatically higher. This is a bold simplification, but it's an extremely powerful mental model to help understand Core Data's performance profile.

At the top of the stack are the managed objects and their context. Whenever we can keep operations inside this tier, performance will be extremely fast. The next tier is the persistent store coordinator with its row cache. And finally, there's the SQL layer and the file system.

The tricky part is that our code will only ever use the top tier, but some operations will indirectly require Core Data to go down to the other tiers.

Let's say we access a property on a managed object (the name property of a Person). If the managed object is fully materialized (it's not a fault), we'll stay within the context tier. In our simple performance model, this will take a single unit of time and/or energy. If the managed object is a fault, but the data exists in the row cache, accessing the property will require dropping into the coordinator tier. As a result, it will be about 10 times as expensive: 10 units of time and/or energy. If the row cache doesn't have this data either, the data has to be retrieved from the SQL store. That will be about 100 times as expensive as the original case: 100 units of time and/or energy.

Again, this performance model is a bold oversimplification, but it illustrates the impact very well. In order to use Core Data, we need our data to be inside the context tier, which is made up of the context and the managed objects. In order to get the data there, we need to drop to the other tiers. In order to optimize performance, we need to limit round trips to these tiers as much as possible. That's the crux of almost all Core Data performance improvements.

Performance in More Detail

The actual numbers are different from the simplified 10× and 100× figures outlined above — these numbers depend a lot on what exactly the application is doing. It's impossible to give precise numbers for a general case, but here's a bit more detail on what goes on in these tiers from a performance perspective.

The managed object context and the managed objects are entirely lock-free because they are only to be accessed from one particular queue. Working within this tier is extremely fast. When a managed object is fully materialized (i.e. it's not a fault), the performance of getting or setting an attribute on a managed object is comparable to the performance of accessing a regular property on a class instance.

When we have to drop into the coordinator tier, the performance characteristics change. The persistent store coordinator is thread-safe. In order for it to be thread-safe, there has to be some locking. If access to the persistent store coordinator is uncontended#Granularity), this is still extremely fast — effectively as fast as an uncontended spinlock.

But when access is contended, the performance can drop dramatically. When two or more managed object contexts use the same persistent store coordinator and try to access the coordinator at the same time, only one of them will be able to access it at any given time. All others will be blocked until the one accessing it is done.

In an uncontended scenario, the cost of pulling data from the coordinator's row cache is close to negligible. However, if we imagine a contended situation where we loop through a collection of managed objects that are all faults, we will continuously drop into the coordinator tier to fulfill the faults. As a result, we'll repeatedly run the risk of being blocked by another context using the persistent store coordinator, and we will also repeatedly block the coordinator from being used by another context. This will degrade the performance of both the context doing this work and other contexts that need to use the same coordinator.

Once we have to drop to the SQL tier, there's another performance shift. Multiple things come into play at this point — there's some locking going on at this layer too. SQLite uses file system locks as a way of ensuring that multiple instances can access the same database file. The performance characteristics of this will vary widely based on whether or not there's contention. Additionally, it is important to remember that SQLite will read data from the file system. Once we execute SQL, we're bound to read data from or write data to the file system. And even on modern systems, accessing the file system is dramatically slower than anything you could do in memory. These are orders of magnitude.

Quite often we get away with decent performance when we execute SQL, because SQLite will cache some data in its so-called page cache. In turn, the operating system will cache some file system data in otherwise unused memory. When the database file is very large, its data may spill out of these caches and SQLite access may become dramatically more expensive than for small databases. In these situations, we need to be particularly careful how we access data.

We will talk about indexes in more detail below. But let's assume we have a very large database that contains a list of products. If we want to find a specific product in the database by its product number, and the database does not have an index for the product number, we can force SQLite to scan through the entire database to find any products that match. If the database file is very large, this will result in a lot of file system access.

Meanwhile, an index allows SQLite to scan the index instead of the data itself. In essence, it's a data structure that is smaller and can be scanned more efficiently. Because of the efficient layout and its compact size, less data has to be transferred from the file system into memory in order to find matching entries. An index can also dramatically improve sorting.

If, however, the database is relatively small (let's assume 200 products), scanning all of these would probably be comparable to scanning the index, because in both cases, the data would fit into the cache of SQLite.

The locking inside the SQL tier is only relevant when we use multiple persistent store coordinators to access the same database, as we'll describe in more detail in the concurrency chapter. Core Data uses SQLite's Write-Ahead Logging (WAL) journaling mode, which minimizes the contention, so reading and writing can proceed concurrently. But there will be some contention — the amount depends on how large the changesets are.

Avoiding Fetch Requests

The biggest performance offenders are fetch requests. Fetch requests have to traverse the entire Core Data stack. By API contract, a fetch request — even though it originates at the managed object context — will consult the SQLite store in the file system.

Because of this, fetch requests are inherently expensive. We'll soon look at how to make sure fetch requests are as cheap as possible, but even though it sounds a bit cheesy, it's still important to point out: the fastest fetch request is the one you don't have to make. Phrased differently: the biggest gain can be made by avoiding fetch requests as much as possible. If there's a single thing to take away from this chapter, this is it.

How to avoid fetch requests depends on the situation at hand. We will take a look at some common patterns: using relationships, and using singleton-like objects.

Relationships

There are a few ways in which actively using relationships can make an app faster. For this section, we will use the following simple model. Assume we have a *City* entity and a *Person* entity with these relationships:

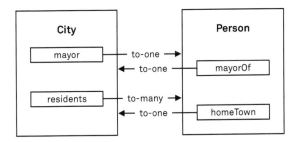

Figure 6.2: The relationships between the *City* and *Person* entities used as an example

Each city has residents and a mayor. A person has a homeTown and can be a mayorOf a city. The latter relationship, mayor and mayorOf, is a one-to-one relationship.

To-One Relationships

If we have a City object and want to get the Person who is the mayor of that city, we have two options: we can either (A) access the mayor attribute on the City object, or (B) execute a fetch request for a Person with a predicate mayorOf == %@. The performance characteristics of these two are very different.

If we access the mayor attribute, two things come into play. First, if the City object is a fault, its data needs to be filled, just as if we had accessed any other attribute of it. Second, once the City object is materialized, the context creates a Person object corresponding to the city's mayor. But this object will also be a fault, unless it has already been accessed.

The last part of this is important to understand. Core Data enforces uniquing. Because of that, if the Person object is already registered with the context, the city's mayor property will point to that instance. And if that Person object is fully materialized (not a fault), the mayor property will point to that fully materialized Person object.

In many applications, some objects are repeatedly used. These objects are likely to already be registered with the context because some other part of the application holds onto them. In such a case, it is a lot cheaper to traverse the relationship than to execute a fetch request.

Again, there are two steps in case (A). The first is obtaining the object ID of the Person — this is done when the City's attributes are obtained. The second is obtaining the attributes of the Person object — this is done once they're accessed.

Contrast this to case (B), where we execute a fetch request. Due to the API contract, the fetch request will *always* work its way through all tiers and interact with the file system to retrieve the data for the corresponding Person object. In case (A), this round trip will only occur if needed.

Case (A) does, however, need to materialize the City object if it's a fault. In case (B), that will not happen.

It should be clear from this that it's quite often the best option to use the relationship and traverse the mayor relationship. If we're using the City object to fill in our UI, it will already be materialized. And traversing the relationship will, in the worst case, be as expensive as the fetch request, but there is a good chance we won't have to drop down to either the coordinator or the SQL tier.

To-Many Relationships

To-many relationships work in a slightly different way: they use two-step faulting.

The City objects have a property called residents, which is a to-many relationship to Person objects. As with to-one relationships, there are two options: (A) access the residents attribute on the City object, or (B) execute a fetch request for Person objects with a predicate homeTown == %@.

The fetch request works in a way similar to the case for a to-one relationship, only that we'll potentially retrieve multiple objects.

What's more interesting is how traversing the relationship behaves. When the City object's attributes are materialized, the residents property turns into a so-called *relationship fault*. And correspondingly, if the City object is a fault, accessing the residents property will materialize the object's attributes. But again, the residents property will still be a relationship fault.

The object that residents returns is the relationship fault. This object is a Set (or an NSSet in Objective-C), but behind the scenes, it delays doing any work. Only when we access the elements or count of this set does Core Data resolve the relationship and fill in the objects that this relationship points to: Core Data will insert the corresponding Person objects into the Set. If the individual Person objects did not already exist in the context, they will all be faults. If some or all of them did already exist (as faults or fully materialized), then those instances are inserted.

The tradeoff for to-many relationships is similar to the tradeoff for to-one relationships.

If the objects at the other end of the relationship are likely to be registered with the context already, it makes more sense to use the relationship, because we won't have to retrieve the object data from SQLite again. If they're less likely to be registered already (particularly if there are a lot of them), it makes more sense to execute a fetch request. As a middle ground, we can ask for the objects in the to-many relationship and then execute a fetch request for only those objects in the relationship that are faults (if any). See the fetchObjectsThatAreFaults() method in the section below on avoiding multiple, consecutive faults.

For example, let's assume we have *Person* and *City* entities. Each person has a to-many visitedCities relationship to City, and we know that we will only have a total of 50 or so cities in our entire object graph. As a result, we could hold all cities in memory using the technique described below under the small datasets section. Going through the visitedCities relationship would then always be faster than executing a fetch request.

Ordered Relationships

Ordered relationships are convenient for some aspects of our model. However, they also represent a performance tradeoff. An ordered relationship is slower when it comes to inserting and updating objects, because Core Data has to manage and persist the order too. An unordered to-many relationship does not need to keep any information about order. But when we want to retrieve objects in a particular order, it is faster to retrieve the pre-ordered data in an ordered relationship than to retrieve the data and then sort it, even if the sorting is done in SQLite as described in the section about sort performance.

Finding a Particular Object

Quite often, particularly in code that works with updates coming in over the network, we need to find a single object that matches a specific predicate. If our backend tells us that an object with a given *remote identifier* has changes or has been deleted, we need to get that object so that we can update or delete it.

Also, in this case, we can often avoid a fetch request. What we'll do is simply check if there's already an object in the context that matches the predicate we're looking for. If so, we'll simply return it; otherwise, we'll execute the fetch request. This works when we know that only one object can match a particular predicate.

We can use this helper method:

```
extension ManagedObjectType where Self: ManagedObject {
    public static func findOrFetchInContext(moc: NSManagedObjectContext,
        matchingPredicate predicate: NSPredicate) -> Self?
    {
        guard let obj = materializedObjectInContext(moc,
            matchingPredicate: predicate)
        else {
            return fetchInContext(moc) { request in
                request.predicate = predicate
                request.returnsObjectsAsFaults = false
                request.fetchLimit = 1
            }. first
        }
        return obj
    }
}
```

This, in turn, uses this method on ManagedObjectType:

```
extension ManagedObjectType where Self: ManagedObject {
    public static func materializedObjectInContext(
        moc: NSManagedObjectContext,
```

```
matchingPredicate predicate: NSPredicate) -> Self?
{
    for obj in moc.registeredObjects where !obj.fault {
        guard let res = obj as? Self
            where predicate.evaluateWithObject(res)
            else { continue }
        return res
    }
    return nil
}
}
```

This small trick can help if the code is likely to request the same object(s) over and over.

Singleton-Like Objects

In many applications, we find ourselves needing a few particular objects very frequently. Let's say we have a *Person* entity and class. If there's one Person who corresponds to the logged-in user, our code will probably access this object frequently from many places.

We could use the code above for finding a particular object. But in this case, we can go even further: we will put the object into the managed object context's userInfo dictionary. This will ensure there's always a strong reference to the object.

Our goal is to have a static method, like the following on the Person class:

```
extension Person {
    static func personForLoggedInUserInContext(
        moc: NSManagedObjectContext) -> Person?
    {
        // ...
    }
}
```

To achieve this, we start by adding two helper methods to NSManagedObjectContext. With these, we can use a cache key to get and set managed objects on the context:

```
private let SingleObjectCacheKey = "SingleObjectCache"
private typealias SingleObjectCache = [String:NSManagedObject]
```

```
extension NSManagedObjectContext {
    public func setObject(object: NSManagedObject?,
        forSingleObjectCacheKey key: String)
    {
        var cache = userInfo[SingleObjectCacheKey] as? SingleObjectCache ?? [:]
        cache[key] = object
        userInfo[SingleObjectCacheKey] = cache
    }

    public func objectForSingleObjectCacheKey(key: String)
        -> NSManagedObject?
    {
        guard let cache = userInfo[SingleObjectCacheKey]
            as? [String:NSManagedObject]
            else { return nil }
        return cache[key]
    }
}
```

Using those helpers, we can define a
fetchSingleObjectInContext(_:cacheKey:configure:) method on our
ManagedObjectType protocol. This method first tries to retrieve the object
from the cache in the context's userInfo. If there's nothing in the cache, it calls
a private method, which actually executes the fetch request:

```
extension ManagedObjectType where Self: ManagedObject {
    public static func fetchSingleObjectInContext(
        moc: NSManagedObjectContext, cacheKey: String,
        configure: NSFetchRequest -> ()) -> Self?
    {
        guard let cached = moc.objectForSingleObjectCacheKey(cacheKey)
            as? Self else
        {
            let result = fetchSingleObjectInContext(moc, configure: configure)
            moc.setObject(result, forSingleObjectCacheKey: cacheKey)
            return result
        }
        return cached
    }

    private static func fetchSingleObjectInContext(
        moc: NSManagedObjectContext, configure: NSFetchRequest -> ())
        -> Self?
    {
```

```
        let result = fetchInContext(moc) { request in
            configure(request)
            request.fetchLimit = 2
        }
        switch result.count {
        case 0: return nil
        case 1: return result[0]
        default: fatalError("Returned multiple objects, expected max 1")
        }
    }
}
```

Now we can implement the personForLoggedInUserInContext(_:) method:

```
extension Person {
    static func personForLoggedInUserInContext(
        moc: NSManagedObjectContext) -> Person?
    {
        return fetchSingleObjectInContext(moc, cacheKey: "loggedInUser") {
            request in
            request.predicate = NSPredicate(format: "self == %@", objectID)
        }
    }
}
```

The objectID of the logged-in user could, for example, be stored in the persistent store's metadata.

The first time personForLoggedInUserInContext(_:) gets called, we still execute the fetch request, and the performance will be the same as before. But on subsequent calls, it is extremely fast. It is important to keep in mind that care must be taken if this object is ever to be deleted. To do so, we would have to clean the cache entries in the userInfo dictionary.

Small Datasets

Another scenario is working with a relatively small dataset. Either you know in advance that the entire number of objects your app will use is limited to a few hundred objects, or you know that a specific entity is limited to a similar number of objects.

If your dataset is small, it may well be worth it to simply load the full dataset into memory once and then operate on it in memory. You can use a single fetch request to pull all objects into the context and then put them into an array so that they remain strongly referenced.

One option is to put this array into the context's userInfo dictionary, but it may make more sense to hold onto the objects somewhere else, such as in a view controller. It all depends on how the app uses those objects and how long it makes sense to keep them around.

When you then need all objects of this particular entity, you can simply use the array created earlier. If you're looking for objects that match a particular predicate, you can filter the array for those objects. Doing this will be very fast for small datasets. The same goes for sorting: if the objects are already in memory (and not faults), in-memory sorting is very fast and efficient.

While these approaches are very good for small datasets, they obviously make no sense at all if you're dealing with thousands or hundreds of thousands of objects.

Optimizing Fetch Requests

There are times when fetch requests are needed. And in those situations, there are still a few things we can do to make sure we get the best performance.

There are two parts about executing fetch requests that are quite expensive. By far, the most expensive one is to look up the data in the SQLite database. The other cost is moving data from the store into the row cache (and eventually to the managed object context).

We have an entire chapter dedicated to predicates. Here, we'll look more specifically at all other aspects of fetch request performance.

Sorting Objects

One thing to note is that SQLite is extremely fast at sorting objects, particularly if things are sorted by an attribute that's indexed. You'll find more on indexes below.

When we get multiple objects from Core Data by means of a fetch request, we will almost always want to display them to the user in a particular order, and it will almost always be best for performance to let SQLite sort the objects by setting the appropriate NSSortDescriptors on the fetch request.

Sorting things after the fact can be slow for many reasons. If you use any of the sort methods on Array or NSArray, these methods will have to access the attributes on each and every managed object in that array. In doing so, they will materialize each and every object. If our intention is to have an array of faults or an array with a batch size (see below), the in-memory sorting will counteract this.

Additionally, an SQLite index on an attribute will allow SQLite to return data that is pre-sorted at almost no cost, compared to an after-the-fact sorting in memory. Be sure to read about indexes below.

Avoiding Multiple, Consecutive Faults

But first, we'll look at a situation where using a fetch request can actually improve performance. If we have multiple objects that are faults and we need to access their properties, it can be expensive to trigger the fault for each object on its own. Materializing all objects in one batch will be faster. We can do this by executing a single fetch request for all objects that we're interested in.

Since Core Data ensures uniquing, we don't need to use the result of such a fetch request. The objects that we're already holding onto will be updated.

For a collection of objects all of the same entity, the following code will execute a fetch request for those objects that are faults:

```
extension CollectionType where Generator.Element: NSManagedObject {
    public func fetchObjectsThatAreFaults() {
        guard !self.isEmpty else { return }
        guard let context = self. first ?.managedObjectContext
            else { fatalError("Managed object must have context") }
        let faults = self. filter  { $0.fault }
        guard let mo = faults.first  else { return }
        let request = NSFetchRequest()
        request.entity = mo.entity
        request.returnsObjectsAsFaults = false
        request.predicate = NSPredicate(format: "self in %@", faults)
        try! context.executeFetchRequest(request)
    }
}
```

We make use of this technique in the table view controller that displays the mood objects. Each table view cell shows the name of the country the mood was captured in. If the table view shows all moods captured on a certain continent, chances are that not all country objects have been loaded before.

We want to avoid having to go back to SQLite for each country fault. Therefore, using the fetchObjectsThatAreFaults() helper shown above, we prefetch the data for the country faults once when the table view controller appears:

```
extension MoodSource {
    func prefetchInContext(context: NSManagedObjectContext)
        -> [MoodyModel.Country]
    {
        switch self {
        case .Continent(let c):
            c.countries.fetchObjectsThatAreFaults()
            return Array(c.countries)
        default: return []
        }
    }
}
```

Fetching in Batches

When using fetched results controllers, you want to set a batch size on the underlying fetch request to only pull in the data that's needed. The request should be configured like this:

```
request.returnsObjectsAsFaults = false
request.fetchBatchSize = <appropriate size>
```

The objects that the fetch request returns will immediately be displayed, so we want their attributes to be populated right away. Without this, the objects would be faults: data would only be pulled into the row cache, and it would only subsequently be pulled into the context as each object's attributes are accessed. We'd pay the price of working with the persistent store coordinator for each object.

Setting the fetch batch size is important for another reason: we limit the amount of data transferred from the store to the persistent store coordinator and the managed object context. This makes quite a difference, particularly for large datasets. Without a batch size, Core Data will move all data for all matching objects into the row cache. Not only does that take up memory, but it also takes time and consumes energy.

When we set a batch size, though, we will incur an additional cost as we move through the dataset: as the user scrolls the table view, we will, at certain intervals, have to fetch new data for the next batch. In setting the batch size appropriately, we ensure that the cost of pulling in each batch is relatively low, and that we don't have to pay this cost too often.

Using Instruments, we can fine-tune the batch size, but quite often, a conservative guess goes a long way. As a rule of thumb, a batch size that's 1.3 times the number of items that fit onto a single screen is a good starting point. It's important to keep in mind that the number of items on a single screen depends on the device. For a table view, simply dividing the screen height by the row height and multiplying by 1.3 will work well, even if the table view effectively ends up being a bit smaller.

Fetched Results Controller

Most of the performance characteristics of the fetched results controller depend directly on the performance of the underlying fetch request. In particular, it is important to make sure that the sorting can use indexes in the SQLite store. We'll talk more about indexes below.

In addition, fetched results controllers can use a persisted cache. The cache helps speed up subsequent uses of the same fetched results controller. Particularly for data that changes less frequently between launches of the app, using such a cache for fetched results controllers that are to be displayed upon launch can help improve launch performance. It also helps when the dataset that the fetched results controller needs to display is large.

Upon creating the fetched results controller, you can pass a cacheName. Doing so tells Core Data to use caching. The name for the given fetch request and section name key path needs to be unique within the app. The documentation for NSFetchedResultsController talks about this in more detail.

Relationship Prefetching

As mentioned above, objects that are returned by a fetch request will by default not have their attributes populated; the data will only be pulled into the row cache. Only when we set returnsObjectsAsFaults to **false** will the objects be fully populated, i.e. not be faults. For relationships, the situation is even more severe. For to-one relationships, the fetch request will retrieve the object ID of the target object as part of the fetch. For to-many relationships, no work will be done.

If we need to access the object at the other end of a relationship, doing so will trigger a fault. For to-many relationships, this will even be a double fault.

In cases where we know that we'll need the objects at the other end of a particular relationship, we can tell the fetch request to prefetch these objects:

```
request.relationshipKeyPathsForPrefetching = ["mayorOf"]
```

We can even do that several levels into the graph by using a key path (i.e. "friends.posts" would prefetch the objects that the "friends" relationship points to, and then for each of those objects, prefetch the objects that the "posts" relationship points to).

However, it is very important to point out that if you need to do relationship prefetching to display rows in a table view, that's a code smell. If this need arises, you should revisit your model and ask yourself if denormalizing the model makes sense. We'll talk more about denormalization below.

Indexes

A managed object model can specify that a given attribute should be indexed, or that a so-called *compound index* should be created for a specific combination of attributes. If so, Core Data will instruct SQLite to create such an index.

Indexes improve performance in two different ways when fetching: they can dramatically improve sorting performance, and they can dramatically improve performance when using a predicate with a fetch request.

It is essential to mention that adding indexes comes at a price: adding and updating data becomes more costly because the index has to be updated. Also, the database file will be bigger because it has to include the indexes too.

Let's assume that we have an entity, *City*, with the population as one of its attributes:

name	population
Berlin	3,562,166
San Francisco	852,469
Beijing	21,516,000
...	

If we're asking Core Data for all cities with a population of more than 1 million, it will in turn ask SQLite to filter the cities to only return those that have a population of 1 million or more. If we don't have an index for the population attribute, the best thing SQLite can do is scan through all cities and check if the population of each one matches.

As SQLite scans through the entire table, it has to make a lot of comparisons: one for each entry. But the other thing that's potentially very expensive is that as it moves through all entries for cities, it will have to dig through a lot of other data in addition to the cities' populations. In doing so, it will have to move a lot of data that's not relevant for checking the population from the file system to memory. That's because the file system (just like SQLite) has its data organized by *pages*, which have to move from the file system as a whole.

If we add an index on the population attribute for the *City* entity, SQLite will create another data structure inside the database. This index will contain data only for the population for all cities. The data structure is laid out in a way that makes it very efficient to either sort by population or find those entries that are larger, smaller, or equal to a particular value. The index is efficient both because of the way it's laid out and because it is more compact.

When we change entries or insert new ones, SQLite also has to update any indexes for the *City* entity, and each index will incur additional costs for changes and inserts.

With this in mind, it's clear that adding an index to an entity is a tradeoff. While it can make lookups faster, it will make the database larger and make changes to the database more expensive. The important thing is to know about these tradeoffs and to measure performance accordingly. It may even make sense to add performance tests for critical paths to avoid regressions.

Whether or not the tradeoff of adding an index will pay off for you depends on how often your application fetches data, compared to how often it changes data. When updates or inserts are very frequent, it may be better not to have an index. If updates and inserts are infrequent, but lookups and searches are very frequent, adding an index may be a good idea.

Another factor is the size of the dataset: when the number of entries for a particular entity is relatively small, adding an index is unlikely to help, since scanning all data is going to be just as fast. However, if the number of entries is very large, it's likely that adding an index will dramatically improve performance.

Compound Indexes

Core Data also supports compound indexes through SQLite. They work for searches or sorting based on a combination of two or more attributes.

Let's assume that our *City* entity has an attribute called isCapital, which is 1 if the city is a capital of a country, and 0 if it's not. We want to sort all cities so that all the capitals are displayed first, with the remaining cities after that. Within each group, cities should be sorted by population.

We could improve the performance of the query (i.e. the fetch request) by adding a normal index for isCapital — the first part of our sort. This would speed things up a bit, but there's a better approach. Instead, we can add a single *compound index* based on both isCapital and population:

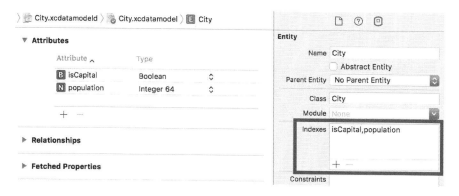

Figure 6.3: Creating a compound index in the Data Model Inspector

The compound index is very efficient for queries that involve both attributes in the order that was specified for the compound index. We can use the compound index for isCapital,population for sorting by isCapital and then population, or just for sorting on isCapital. If we want to sort on population, we cannot use this compound index.

Just as with single attribute indexes, we need to keep in mind that compound indexes increase the database size. When adding a compound index, it is important to check if indexes on a single attribute overlap these. Having two indexes — a compound index on isCapital,population, and another index on the single attribute isCapital — doesn't improve fetch performance when compared to just having a compound index on isCapital,population. But having both the compound and the single attribute index will require SQLite to update both indexes whenever there are changes, and updates will become more expensive. For a given fetch request, SQLite will only be able to use a single index due to the way the SQLite query planner[1] is implemented.

For large databases and complex and frequent queries, a compound index may make sense. But in the end, only profiling your specific use case can give you a definitive answer.

Be sure to refer to the chapter on profiling to learn how to check if SQLite uses any indexes that you add to your model for specific fetch requests. That chapter explains how to use the SQLite EXPLAIN QUERY PLAN command, which gives insights into how SQLite searches and sorts data.

Inserting and Changing Objects

Inserting and changing are conceptually the opposite of a fetch request. Data moves from the managed object context, all the way through the stack, down to the store, and for inserts, new object identifiers move back into the managed object context.

It is important to note, though, that inserting new objects into the context, or changing existing objects are both very cheap — these operations only touch the managed object context. Inserts and changes all operate within the context without touching the SQLite tier.

Only when these changes are being saved to the store is the cost relatively high. A save operation involves both the coordinator tier and the SQL tier. As such, a call to save() is rather expensive.

1 https://www.sqlite.org/queryplanner.html

The key takeaway is quite simply to reduce the number of saves. But there's a balance to strike: saving a very large number of changes increases the memory usage because the context has to keep track of these changes until they're saved. And processing a large change requires more CPU and memory than a smaller one. However, in total, a large changeset is cheaper than many small ones.

A very important consideration is how long the main context and the main thread/queue can be busy. Depending on your specific Core Data setup, the main context will be busy due to saves for one of the following reasons:

1. The main context itself is saving changes.

   Depending on the problem at hand, it might be okay to block the main thread for a relatively long period, compared to the 16 ms required for a 60 Hz refresh rate. If the save does not happen while the user otherwise interacts with the UI, it may be OK to spend 20–30 ms. This is very domain specific. And quite often, changesets on the main queue are small: the user will be changing or inserting a single object or just a handful of objects, followed by a save.

2. A non-main queue context saves, and these changes are being merged into the main context.

   This happens when a background (private queue) context does some work, which may very well be while the user is interacting with the UI. The *context-did-save* notification will be merged into the main queue's context, and this merging will happen on the main thread. If the background context performs a very big save, the main context will have to do a lot of work, which will block the main thread.

We'll talk more about different Core Data setups and their tradeoffs in the chapter about complex setups and concurrency.

Also, as we've mentioned in the chapter about changing and saving data, it is worth noting that the save() method is transactional.

How to Build Efficient Data Models

It is tempting to split the model into many entities. But often, the opposite is best for performance.

When creating a data model, the best approach is to look at how data is presented to the user. For a table view, it is best to create the data model so that all data needed to display a single cell is contained within a single entity.

If data for a single cell is split up among multiple entities, Core Data has to fetch multiple objects to display a single cell. That's more expensive, and there's a fixed per-object cost. The cost of large objects compared to smaller objects is mostly negligible when it comes to executing fetch requests.

One-to-one relationships can often be inlined. In a model with a *Person* and a *Pet* entity, and a one-to-one relationship between them (owner/pet), we could also inline this information into a single entity — PersonWithPet — that has both personName and petName.

Another trick is *denormalization*: if our model represents an address book, where a *Person* entity can have one or two street addresses, it may seem obvious to have a *StreetAddress* entity with a relationship between the two. But another option is to inline this information into the *Person* entity. Whether or not this makes sense depends on the specific scenario. But it's worthwhile to think about if the dataset is large and performance is critical.

Another common case for denormalization is the following: let's assume we have a model that has employees and relationships between them to represent who is managed by whom. If we want to show employees in a table view, and for each cell, show the name of an employee alongside the number of other employees reporting to this employee, we could use the naive approach and look at the to-many relationship to count the number of objects. However, this would be quite expensive, since a relationship fault would have to be fulfilled for each employee.

Another option is to put the number of team members reporting to an employee into that employee's object. The *Employee* entity would have a teamMembers relationship and a numberOfTeamMembers attribute. This is effectively data duplication, or in database lingo, denormalization. We've been taught time and time again that data duplication is bad, but in this case, it can be an extremely powerful tool to improve fetch performance.

The important thing when applying this kind of trick is to make sure that the model class automatically updates the duplicated attributes, and that they appear as read-only to the rest of your application.

We also use this technique in the *Moody* sample app. In the table view that displays the continents and countries, we show the number of moods contained within a certain country or continent as well. For example, a table view cell representing a country would have a detail label saying "42 moods." Similarly, in a cell representing a continent, we would state "42 moods in 7 countries."

In order to avoid having to prefetch the countries and moods relationships, we use the approach outlined above: we introduce data duplication in our data model by adding a *numberOfMoods* attribute to the *Country* and *Continent* entities, as well as a *numberOfCountries* attribute to the *Continent* entity. To keep those attributes up to date, we hook into the managed object's willSave() method. For example, in the Country class, we check if the moods relationship has changed and update the numberOfMoods property accordingly:

```
public final class Country: ManagedObject {
    // ...
    public override func willSave() {
        // ...
        if hasChangedMoods {
            updateMoodCount()
        }
    }

    private var hasChangedMoods: Bool {
        return changedValueForKey(Keys.Moods) != nil
    }

    private func updateMoodCount() {
        guard Int64(moods.count) != numberOfMoods else { return }
        numberOfMoods = Int64(moods.count)
        continent?.updateMoodCount()
    }
}
```

In hasChangedMoods, we call the helper method changedValueForKey(_:) to check whether or not the moods relationship has unsaved changes. This helper uses Core Data's changedValues() method under the hood. Within updateMoodCount(), we first check whether the number of moods really has changed and exit early if not. This is important in order to avoid dirtying the country object again and again, causing an infinite loop during saving. Then we set the new number of moods on the numberOfMoods property, and lastly, we tell the country's continent to refresh its mood count as well.

The updateMoodCount() method in the Continent class is a bit more complicated, since continents don't have a direct relationship to moods. We have to ask each related country for its unsaved change in number of moods and sum up those results. However, we also need to take into account that countries might have been deleted. Therefore, we have to consult not only the currently related countries, but also those that have been removed from the countries relationship:

```
public final class Continent: ManagedObject {
    // ...
    func updateMoodCount() {
        let currentAndDeletedCountries = countries.union(committedCountries)
        let deltaInCountries: Int64 = currentAndDeletedCountries.reduce(0) {
            $0 + $1.changedMoodCountDelta
        }
        let pendingDelta = numberOfMoods - committedNumberOfMoods
        guard pendingDelta != deltaInCountries else { return }
        numberOfMoods = committedNumberOfMoods + deltaInCountries
    }

    private var committedCountries: Set<Country> {
        return committedValueForKey(Keys.Countries) as? Set<Country> ?? Set()
    }

    private var committedNumberOfMoods: Int64 {
        let n = committedValueForKey(Keys.NumberOfMoods) as? Int ?? 0
        return Int64(n)
    }
}
```

Again, before setting numberOfMoods, we have to make sure that the value has actually changed, in order to avoid dirtying the continent object unnecessarily.

> When working with Core Data's changedValues() and committedValuesForKeys(_:) methods, you're usually using plain strings to get to the values you want. We're wrapping those methods with type-safe helpers that only accept values of a Keys enum. An additional benefit is that we now get autocompletion when working with those keys. The code is available on GitHub[a].
>
> ───────────
> a https://github.com/objcio/core-data/blob/master/SharedCode/KeyCodable.swift

Getting the code for keeping denormalized attributes up to date can be somewhat tricky and is a good candidate for automatic tests. You can find the tests for the numberOfMoods and numberOfCountries attributes in the sample code[2].

Strings and Text

The performance related to working with strings and text is a topic that we have dedicated an entire chapter to.

Esoteric Tunables

The underlying SQLite library provides quite a few tunable parameters that can be set through so-called pragmas. When using Core Data and calling addPersistentStoreWithType(_:configuration:URL:options:), these pragmas need to be passed as options by setting them as a dictionary for the NSSQLitePragmasOption key.

In combination, Core Data and SQLite use some very reasonable default values, but for specific use cases, it is worthwhile to consult the SQLite documentation for PRAGMA Statements[3].

For applications that depend on a large number of writes, it may be worth investigating the performance of turning off automatic checkpointing and instead manually checkpointing the database at idle moments. This can be done with the wal_autocheckpoint and database.wal_checkpoint pragmas. If your application falls into this group, you should also check how switching the journaling mode from WAL to Atomic Commit[4] affects performance.

Summary

In this chapter, we introduced a mental performance model of Core Data by splitting the stack into three tiers: the context tier, the coordinator tier, and the SQLite tier. We then discussed how fetch requests are generally expensive,

2 https://github.com/objcio/core-data/blob/master/Moody/MoodyModelTests/DenormalizationTests.swift
3 https://www.sqlite.org/pragma.html
4 https://www.sqlite.org/draft/atomiccommit.html

and how to avoid them in many situations. Next, we took a look at how to make sure fetch requests perform well when we need them. Most of this chapter is about trying to stay within the context tier whenever possible, and how to ensure that SQLite can do its work as efficiently as possible whenever we actually need to drop down to the SQLite tier.

Part 3
Concurrency
and Syncing

Syncing with a Network Service

Many apps sync their local data with a backend, and we want to illustrate an approach that works well as a generic setup for these scenarios. One of the key design goals of our syncing architecture is to ensure a clear separation of concerns, i.e. small parts that each have a very limited responsibility.

The *Moody* example app uses this setup for its specific syncing needs. We hope that the sample code helps you understand how we intend for the synching architecture to be put to use.

Throughout this chapter, the words *local* and *remote* have very specific meanings: *local* refers to things originating on a device, whereas *remote* refers to things originating on a server, which, in our case, is CloudKit. A local change, hence, is a change that originates on a device, e.g. a change caused by a user action, such as creating a new mood. Correspondingly, the term *remote identifier* refers to the identifier that CloudKit uses for a given object. Using the words *local* and *remote* throughout the code and this chapter simplifies a lot of the terminology.

This chapter will go less into detail and actual code samples and instead mostly try to convey the big picture of how to put together a code base that can sync local data with a backend. The *Moody* app on GitHub[1] has the full code for a relatively simple implementation of this. Once you have read this chapter, the example project is a good place to look for more details.

Organization and Setup

We will use CloudKit as our backend for the example app. That's mainly because the purpose of the example is to showcase Core Data and not to write a backend. Using CloudKit, we can share Mood instances between all users of the app without having to write our own backend. Plus we can keep our focus on Core Data. However, the architecture and code we describe here will work for more complex situations as well. Toward the end of this chapter, we will further discuss some ways to expand the shown setup depending on your needs.

All the CloudKit-specific code is encapsulated in the CloudKitRemote struct, which implements the MoodyRemoteType protocol. This protocol exposes all the domain-specific functionality we need to communicate with the remote.

---

1 https://github.com/objcio/core-data

For the sake of simplicity, we'll mostly ignore the MoodyRemoteType abstraction and just talk about CloudKit as our remote.

The sample project uses a dummy remote by default, which only logs to the console (ConsoleRemote). This makes it easier to get the project running, because you don't have to worry about app entitlements and provisioning profiles. The steps to enable the CloudKit remote are described in the sample project's README file[2].

As for the CloudKit code in the sample app, we do not intend this to be a state-of-the-art CloudKit implementation. In fact, we are skipping a lot of CloudKit details, as our focus is clearly on the Core Data side of the sync architecture. Please keep this in mind when browsing through the complete code[3] on GitHub.

Project Structure

As we're adding the sync code, we want to put it into its own framework and module. We'll also move all model code into a separate model framework. This framework will hold all our custom NSManagedObject subclasses and their related logic that's not specific to the UI or syncing.

We end up with three modules in total: the app itself, the model, and the sync code. This setup facilitates a clear separation of concerns on a high level — we're less tempted to create a tight coupling between any of these three modules:

2 https://github.com/objcio/core-data/blob/master/README.md
3 https://github.com/objcio/core-data

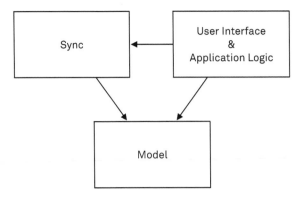

Figure 7.1: Breaking up the sample app into three modules: the application logic, the model, and the syncing engine

The interface of the sync framework will be quite small. The entry point for the sync code is a sync coordinator class that gets initialized with a managed object context:

```
public final class SyncCoordinator {
    public init (
        mainManagedObjectContext mainMOC: NSManagedObjectContext)
    {
        // ...
    }
}
```

In our simple app, the application delegate is in charge of creating the sync coordinator.

The sync code works in the background on its own private background queue and context, which we'll discuss shortly. All updates to the UI will work with the reactive approach that we introduced earlier: the UI simply observes changes to its context or objects. Only minimal additional code changes have to be made to the UI code for features like remote deletion. We'll mention these changes below.

Syncing Architecture

Our syncing architecture is rather generic. It can be used for both simple and complex situations. It tries to split the problem of syncing into small, approachable components. This architecture utilizes the design of Core Data, and it provides a very flexible structure.

Core Data, in conjunction with SQLite, provides ACID properties: Atomicity, Consistency, Isolation, Durability. This sync architecture tries to bring some of these properties to the entire sync process. The sync code is constructed in such a way that it can survive if the app crashes or gets suspended by the OS. Even if we happen to be offline, our local data will remain consistent, and we'll be able to pick up work once the app is relaunched or the network is back online.

The overall setup is sketched below. There's a *Context Owner* protocol (at the bottom of the diagram), which is implemented by the *Sync Coordinator*. The *Context Owner* protocol has two main responsibilities: it merges changes between the UI and the sync managed object context, and it feeds local changes made by the UI into the sync architecture.

The *Sync Coordinator* ties all the pieces together. It owns the Core Data context, the remote interface (implementing MoodyRemoteType), and the change processors. It implements the *Context Owner* protocol. Both local and remote updates are forwarded by the *Sync Coordinator* to the change processors.

The change processors (on the right-hand side) contain domain-specific knowledge. Each one is only responsible for a single kind of change, e.g. creating newly inserted Mood objects on the remote. In our case, we do not have a *Transport Session* to contain the network-specific code because CloudKit handles the encoding and decoding and the generation of network requests for us.

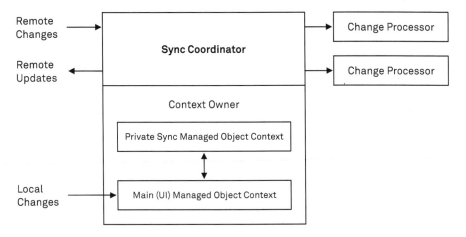

Figure 7.2: The components of the syncing architecture

Context Owner

When the UI saves changes to objects, we want the sync code to pick up these changes automatically. At the same time, we want the sync code to run on a queue different from the one the UI code uses. This is to minimize the impact on UI responsiveness. The *Context Owner* has these two responsibilities.

Threading, Queues, and Context

The goal of the sync architecture is to be single threaded in order to dramatically reduce complexity. At the same time, the architecture ensures that the main queue is left to the UI. As a result, it minimizes the impact on the performance of the UI code.

The context owner achieves this by creating a separate managed object context, which the entire sync code uses. By calling performBlock(_:), all code runs on this managed object context's private queue, thereby not blocking the UI.

Building the sync code as a single-threaded architecture is an important design decision: the performance of the sync code is limited mainly by the speed of network requests and, in a distant second place, by file system I/O. Multithreading would not make any difference for either of these. What a single-threaded architecture buys us, though, is a very straightforward code base — a code base that is very easy to reason about and test.

The chapter on complex and concurrent setups talks in more detail about all the things to be aware of when using multiple contexts. For our sync code, we use our recommended setup, where the UI managed object context and the sync managed object context share a single common persistent store coordinator:

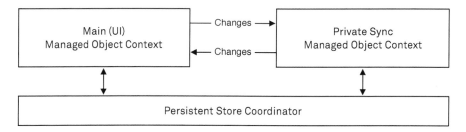

Figure 7.3: The interaction between the main context and the background sync context

Since we're using two contexts, we need to merge changes between them. Changes inside the Core Data stack will not automatically propagate from the persistent store coordinator up to the managed object context. By merging changes between the two contexts, both contexts will update themselves from the persistent store coordinator as changes are merged into them. We explain all of this in more detail in the chapter about complex and concurrent setups.

The context owner protocol implements this merging through a protocol extension with the following code:

```
private func setupContextNotificationObserving() {
    addObserverToken(
        mainManagedObjectContext.addContextDidSaveNotificationObserver {
            [weak self] note in
            self?.mainContextDidSave(note)
        }
    )
    addObserverToken(
        syncManagedObjectContext.addContextDidSaveNotificationObserver {
            [weak self] note in
            self?.syncContextDidSave(note)
        }
    )
```

```
}

/// Merge changes from main -> sync context.
private func mainContextDidSave(note: ContextDidSaveNotification) {
    syncManagedObjectContext
        .performMergeChangesFromContextDidSaveNotification(note)
}

/// Merge changes from sync -> main context.
private func syncContextDidSave(note: ContextDidSaveNotification) {
    mainManagedObjectContext
        .performMergeChangesFromContextDidSaveNotification(note)
}
```

It also implements the following extension on the managed object context:

```
extension NSManagedObjectContext {
    public func performMergeChangesFromContextDidSaveNotification(
        note: ContextDidSaveNotification)
    {
        performBlock {
            self.mergeChangesFromContextDidSaveNotification(
                note.notification)
        }
    }
}
```

With this, when the UI saves changes, they are propagated into the managed object context that the sync code uses. And when the sync code saves its managed object context, those changes are propagated into the managed object context that the UI uses.

Since the UI code listens for NSManagedObjectContextObjectsDidChange notifications to update its UI components, any changes made by the sync code will automatically be reflected there.

Reacting to Local Changes

There are two sources for local changes: both the UI and the sync code can insert or update data. In either case, the change processors are responsible for acting upon changes, and one key design goal is that we do not differentiate as to where the change originated from, nor do we differentiate between insert and update events.

This may seem counterintuitive at first, but it lets us simplify the overall logic, and it allows us to build a system that is consistent if the app gets suspended by the OS or even if it crashes.

Let's take a look at what happens when the user creates a new Mood object locally and we need to send it to the backend: the UI inserts a new Mood object and saves its context, and there's a change processor called MoodUploader that is responsible for sending a request to insert the corresponding object in CloudKit. If we would trigger this upload based on the fact that the object was inserted, and if the app would quit before this insertion completed (maybe our network is slow), then we would not be able to figure out upon relaunch that the object was "recently inserted."

Instead, what we do is this: each change processor has a predicate and an entity. Whenever an object is either inserted or updated, the sync coordinator will forward the object to the change processor, which will then check if the given object matches the combination of entity and predicate. If so, it will act upon the object. Upon relaunch of the app, we perform a fetch request based on the same entity and predicate to see if there are any objects we didn't complete the last time the app ran.

It is very important to refrain from the temptation to base logic upon the distinction between inserts and updates. Instead, we must design our logic in such a way that objects match a given predicate if they are to be considered newly inserted and they need to be uploaded to our backend.

In the case of MoodUploader, it will only match the *Mood* entity, and we use a predicate to detect if objects need to be uploaded:

```
let notUploaded = NSPredicate(format: "%K == NULL", RemoteIdentifierKey)
```

Any Mood object that does not yet have a remote identifier will be sent to CloudKit. Once CloudKit confirms the insert into iCloud, we will set the remote identifier on the Mood object, and that will cause the Mood object to no longer match the predicate.

We use the same approach for the MoodRemover change processor. It will match based on if pendingRemoteDeletion is set, and it will then send requests to CloudKit. Upon success, the object is removed from the local database.

The context owner subscribes to NSManagedObjectContextDidSave notifications and uses these to figure out if any objects have been inserted or updated. It forwards the union of inserted and updated objects to the sync coordinator, which, in turn, distributes these to the change processors. We can ignore deleted objects due to the way we will handle local object deletion. This is described in more detail below when we discuss deleting local objects.

When we receive a did-save notification, we call notifyAboutChangedObjectsFromSaveNotification(_:), which, in turn, calls processChangedLocalObjects(_:). That method will then distribute the objects to all change processors:

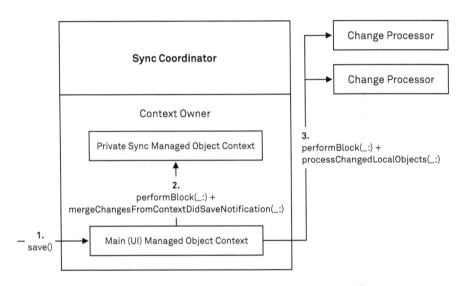

Figure 7.4: The syncing architecture processes local changes in response to merging the main context into the sync context

The code for this looks like the following:

```
private func notifyAboutChangedObjectsFromSaveNotification(
    note: ContextDidSaveNotification)
{
    syncManagedObjectContext.performBlockWithGroup(syncGroup) {
        // We unpack the notification here, to make sure it's retained
        // until this point.
        let updates = note.updatedObjects
            .remapToContext(self.syncManagedObjectContext)
        let inserts = note.insertedObjects
            .remapToContext(self.syncManagedObjectContext)
        self.processChangedLocalObjects(updates + inserts)
```

```
        }
    }

extension SyncCoordinator: ContextOwnerType {
    func processChangedLocalObjects(objects: [NSManagedObject]) {
        for cp in changeProcessors {
            cp.processChangedLocalObjects(objects, context: self)
        }
    }
}
```

We will go into more detail about this in the complex and concurrent setups chapter, but we cannot use objects from one context on a queue different from that context's queue. As we're potentially moving this notification and its objects from one queue to another, we need to make sure to remap the objects to the sync managed object context. We will have to do this once we're on that context's queue.

If the save was on the sync managed object context, this doesn't change anything. If the notification originated from the UI, the objects in the notification belong to the UI managed object context. The remapToContext(_:) method will then take each object's object ID and create the corresponding object on the sync managed object context using the objectWithID(_:) method:

```
extension SequenceType where Generator.Element: NSManagedObject {
    func remapToContext(context: NSManagedObjectContext)
        -> [Generator.Element]
    {
        return map { unmappedMO in
            guard unmappedMO.managedObjectContext !== context
                else { return unmappedMO }
            guard let object = context.objectWithID(unmappedMO.objectID)
                as? Generator.Element
                else { fatalError("Invalid  object type") }
            return object
        }
    }
}
```

One thing to note here is that we do this mapping once we've switched onto the sync managed object context. We keep a strong reference to the original notification, which, in turn, keeps the original objects around. Only when we're on the sync managed object context do we extract the object ID from the original objects and create the new objects. Because we keep a strong reference to the original objects up to this point, the objects will keep a strong reference to their row cache entries. The newly created objects in the sync managed object context will then also retain the same row cache entries, and triggering any faults is a relatively cheap operation.

Reacting to Remote Changes

Since we're using CloudKit, the actual code that deals with changes in the cloud is very specific to it, but the overall concept works for other setups too. When the sync coordinator receives a notification that there are remote changes, it switches onto the queue of the sync managed object context and forwards the changes to all change processors:

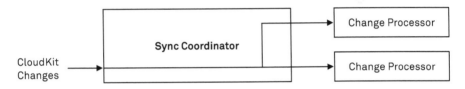

Figure 7.5: CloudKit notifications trigger the sync coordinator, which, in turn, asks its change processors to fetch the latest data

CloudKit passes in a completion handler that our code must run when all changes have been processed. The sync coordinator passes a completion block to each change processor, and the change processors run the completion blocks once they're done with their work. When all change processors have run their completion blocks, the CloudKit completion handler will be called. This lets CloudKit know that the given updates have been processed.

The key thing to get right here is that the sync coordinator and its change processors must do all work on the queue of its managed object context. Callbacks and notifications from CloudKit may come in on another queue. We must be diligent to switch onto the correct queue.

Change Processors

The change processors are the only pieces of the sync architecture that have domain-specific knowledge. The *Moody* example app only has three change processors: MoodDownloader, MoodUploader, and MoodRemover. Each one of these has a very specific task: to download new moods from the cloud, to upload new moods to the cloud, and to remove moods from the cloud, respectively. As a result, their logic is relatively simple.

Also, since the sync coordinator and its other components manage the complexity of threading and tracking remote and local changes, each change processor's task is even further simplified.

The interface of the change processor has two main methods: one to notify of local changes in the Core Data database, and one to notify of remote changes in the cloud. The sync coordinator does not have any knowledge about which changes are relevant for a given change processor. That knowledge lies within the change processor.

The two methods for local and remote changes, respectively, are the following:

```
func processChangedLocalObjects(objects: [NSManagedObject],
    context: ChangeProcessorContextType)
func processChangedRemoteObjects<T: RemoteRecordType>(
    changes: [RemoteRecordChange<T>],
    context: ChangeProcessorContextType, completion: () -> ())
```

The sync coordinator passes a reference of itself to the change processor. It does so as a *change processor context*, which allows the change processor to access the sync coordinator's managed object context and the network interface.

At startup, the sync coordinator needs to make sure that the change processors can retrieve any local or remote objects that still have to be sent to or retrieved from the cloud. For this, the change processors expose these two methods:

```
func entityAndPredicateForLocallyTrackedObjectsInContext(
    context: ChangeProcessorContextType) -> EntityAndPredicate?
func fetchLatestRemoteRecordsForContext(
    context: ChangeProcessorContextType)
```

The sync coordinator uses the first method to execute fetch requests for any objects in the database that are relevant for the change tracker, and it then passes these through the processChangedLocalObjects(_:context:) method. The fetchLatestRemoteRecordsForContext(_:) method is used by the change tracker to fetch new remote objects.

Since change trackers usually operate on a single entity and class, the subprotocol ElementChangeProcessorType makes it simpler to implement a change processor. It tracks which objects are already in progress so that objects don't create duplicate requests to CloudKit, it does type-safe casting of the objects to the specific class that the change processor operates on, and it implements the entityAndPredicateForLocallyTrackedObjectsInContext(_:) method by means of the predicateForLocallyTrackedElements property.

The tracking of objects in progress is implemented by the InProgressTracker helper class. In essence, this class keeps a set of objects that are in progress, and the change processor notifies it when requests for a given object start and complete.

Uploading Moods

As a concrete example, let's take a look at the MoodUploader change processor. It is responsible for uploading new moods added on a user's device to iCloud.

It implements the ElementChangeProcessorType protocol with this code:

```
final class MoodUploader: ElementChangeProcessorType {
    var elementsInProgress = InProgressTracker<Mood>()

    func setupForContext(context: ChangeProcessorContextType) {
        // no-op
    }

    func processChangedLocalElements(objects: [Mood],
        context: ChangeProcessorContextType)
    {
        processInsertedMoods(objects, context: context)
    }

    func processChangedRemoteObjects<T: RemoteRecordType>(
        changes: [RemoteRecordChange<T>],
        context: ChangeProcessorContextType, completion: () -> ())
    {
        // no-op
        completion()
    }

    func fetchLatestRemoteRecordsForContext(
        context: ChangeProcessorContextType)
```

```
    {
        // no-op
    }

    var predicateForLocallyTrackedElements: NSPredicate {
        return Mood.waitingForUploadPredicate
    }
}
```

Most methods of the ElementChangeProcessorType are empty. This change
processor is only concerned with uploads and does not need to handle any
remote data. Note that predicateForLocallyTrackedElements specifies which
local objects this change processor is interested in: those that do not yet have a
remote identifier.

Any objects that MoodUploader needs to insert remotely are then passed to the
processInsertedMoods(_:context:) method, which sends these moods to
CloudKit:

```
extension MoodUploader {
    private func processInsertedMoods(insertions: [Mood],
        context: ChangeProcessorContextType)
    {
        context.remote.uploadMoods(insertions,
            completion: context.performGroupedBlock { remoteMoods, error in

                guard !(error?.isPermanent ?? false) else {
                    // Since the error was permanent, delete these objects:
                    insertions.forEach { $0.markForLocalDeletion() }
                    self.elementsInProgress.markObjectsAsComplete(insertions)
                    return
                }

                for mood in insertions {
                    guard let remoteMood = remoteMoods.findFirstOccurence({
                        mood.date == $0.date
                    }) else { continue }
                    mood.remoteIdentifier = remoteMood.id
                    mood.creatorID = remoteMood.creatorID
                }
                context.delayedSaveOrRollback()
                self.elementsInProgress.markObjectsAsComplete(insertions)
            })
    }
}
```

The change processor context has a remote object. This object encapsulates the CloudKit-specific code. The CloudKit remote's uploadMoods(_:completion:) method creates a *modify records* operation and passes that to CloudKit to execute.

When the upload completes, the method checks for failures. When inserting a Mood into iCloud fails permanently, we simply delete the failing Mood locally. If the upload succeeds, we add the remote identifier that CloudKit returned to us to that Mood.

Deleting Local Objects

In the *Moody* example app, we allow users to delete the Mood instance they have created. But when the user deletes a Mood in the UI, we cannot simply call deleteObject(_:) on the managed object context. If we did, the object would be gone, and no change tracker would be able to tell CloudKit to delete the corresponding object in iCloud.

Instead, we'll add a boolean pendingRemoteDeletion attribute to the *Mood* entity. The UI will simply set this flag, and the defaultPredicate of the Mood class will filter out objects that have this attribute set.

The MoodRemover change processor will then match these objects, send a request to CloudKit to delete them, and upon success, delete the corresponding objects in the local database.

Groups and Saving Changes

The change processors will insert and update objects in the managed object context, mainly as the result of a response from CloudKit. For example, the MoodUploader will send a new Mood object to CloudKit. When CloudKit responds, the MoodUploader change processor will set the remoteIdentifier of the Mood object that was just sent.

These changes need to be saved to the Core Data database. At the same time, we want to limit the number of saves. Particularly in larger setups, it can be beneficial to group multiple changes for a single call to save().

In the *Moody* example app, we use a rather straightforward solution: any work that the sync code executes on its managed object context gets added to a

dispatch group. When a piece of code performs changes, it calls
delayedSaveOrRollback() instead of saveOrRollback().

The *delayed* save simply waits for the group to be empty before it saves. Once
that occurs, it uses dispatch_group_notify(_:_:_:) to execute the save. This way,
as long as the sync code is busy, saves will get delayed. Only once the managed
object context no longer has any work will it save.

We do this with the following extension:

```
extension NSManagedObjectContext {
    private var changedObjectsCount: Int {
        return insertedObjects.count + updatedObjects.count +
            deletedObjects.count
    }

    func delayedSaveOrRollbackWithGroup(group: dispatch_group_t,
        completion: (Bool) -> () = { _ in })
    {
        let changeCountLimit = 100
        guard changeCountLimit >= changedObjectsCount else {
            return completion(saveOrRollback())
        }
        let queue = dispatch_get_global_queue(QOS_CLASS_DEFAULT, 0)
        dispatch_group_notify(group, queue) {
            self.performBlockWithGroup(group) {
                guard self.hasChanges else { return completion(true) }
                completion(self.saveOrRollback())
            }
        }
    }
}
```

In order to run blocks on the managed object context with a group, we extend
NSManagedObjectContext to have a performBlockWithGroup(_:block:) method:

```
extension NSManagedObjectContext {
    func performBlockWithGroup(group: dispatch_group_t, block: () -> ()) {
        dispatch_group_enter(group)
        performBlock {
            block()
            dispatch_group_leave(group)
        }
    }
}
```

The sync coordinator owns the *sync group* and adds these two convenience methods, which are exposed to the change processors as part of the context type, ChangeProcessorContextType:

```
protocol ChangeProcessorContextType: class {
    func performGroupedBlock(block: () -> ())
    func delayedSaveOrRollback()
}
```

Expanding the Sync Architecture

The code in the *Moody* example app is relatively simple. An app with more complex needs would have to expand upon this.

Tracking Per-Attribute Changes

The example app has immutable Mood objects. Once they're inserted, they will never change. However, other apps may need to sync changes on a per-attribute level.

One approach to tracking local changes that still have to be synced to the backend is to add a per-attribute bitmask to each object. This bitmask will not be visible to UI code, but inside the object's willSave() method, the object can check the keys of its changedValues() and set the corresponding bits. This is most easily done through a markAttributeAsLocallyChangedForKey(_:) method that updates the bitmask for a given key.

We only want to do this on the UI context. We can mark a context as the UI context by setting a specific property inside that context's userInfo dictionary. Inside willSave(), we can then check if the object's managed object context is the UI context or not.

Inside the sync code, we need a corresponding method, unmarkAttributeAsLocallyChangedForKey(_:), which the change processor calls once it has pushed the change for a given attribute to the backend.

Chaining Change Processors

It can be useful to chain change processors, and we can do this without any changes to the architecture. If change processor A needs to process objects before change processor B gets a go at them, we need to make sure that B does not match them until A is done.

Let's assume an example where we have one change processor that can set a name on a photo, and another one that can set a rating on a photo. Meanwhile, our backend only allows setting a rating once the photo has a name. For this to work, we just need to make sure that the change processor in charge of ratings will only match objects that have a name that has no local changes — in addition to having local changes to the rating. With this, if we have an object with both a new name and a new rating set on it, the name change processor will match that object, but the rating change processor will not. Only once the name has been sent to the backend will it no longer have local changes, and at that point, the change processor in charge of ratings will pick it up.

Once the name processor is done, it will mark the name as not having local changes. Marking the object and saving it will cause an update for this object to be sent out to all change processors again, and the rating change processors will pick up the object at that point because it matches.

The delayed saving we talked about above can introduce a slight delay between one change processor finishing and the next one picking up the work. This delay is usually negligible compared to other timing aspects such as network latencies because the sync coordinator will be idle quite frequently.

Custom Network Code

For an app that interfaces with a custom backend, using NSURLSession directly instead of a CloudKit-based backend, we would also need to make a few changes.

For such a setup, it makes sense to have a network session class that abstracts both the encoding (to and from JSON) and the sending of HTTP requests. Adding this layer between NSURLSession and the sync coordinator makes it easier to test individual components, and it separates concerns.

If the app potentially has a lot of requests in flight at the same time, it may be worth slightly changing the flow from changed objects to network requests. In the *Moody* app, a changed object will create a CloudKit request directly, and this is sent to CloudKit immediately. It is then up to CloudKit to enqueue this request as it sees fit. If these requests have large payloads and there are many requests, this could potentially cause memory pressure.

How to approach this problem depends on the capabilities of the backend. If the backend supports HTTP/2, the correct approach is to send all requests to the NSURLSession as soon as possible and set their priorities appropriately. The priority ensures that requests are processed in the desired order, both locally and on the remote server. In most cases, it makes sense to use the position of the change processor in the sync coordinator's array as the priority of the requests. If there are four change processors, the sync coordinator will set the priority of requests from these change processors to 1.0, 0.75, 0.5, and 0.25, respectively. The NSURLSession and the HTTP/2-capable backend will then correctly utilize the available resources, both local and remote, to make sure that requests from the first change processor are sent and received at a higher priority than those of the other change processors.

With this setup, if payloads can be large, the network session should use the file-based API to make sure that body data sent and received does not have to reside in memory. This approach will also allow you to take advantage of background sessions.

Another approach, which works better for HTTP/1.1 backends, is to expand the sync architecture and have a local limit on the number of concurrent requests. However, we will still want to prioritize requests, such that each change processor has an implicit priority associated with it. We can achieve this by adding a queue of *pending objects* to each change processor. Whenever the sync coordinator pushes local changes to the change processors, these will simply add matching objects to their queues. As before, these queues are simply in-memory representations of all objects in the database that the given change processor is interested in, i.e. those objects that match its entity and predicate.

The sync coordinator will then use an *operation loop*, which will query all change processors in turn if they have a request they want to send to the *network session*. Once the limit of concurrent operations has been reached, the loop waits for operations to complete, and the queries all change processors again. Since the operation loop asks change processors in their specified order, the higher-priority change processors will get a chance to enqueue the network requests first.

Working with Multiple Contexts

8

In this chapter, we'll look at more complex Core Data setups; in particular, we'll explore how you can use Core Data in a multithreaded environment. Core Data allows for a multitude of different setups, so we'll walk through the advantages and disadvantages of several of these approaches.

In part one of the book, we used the simplest version of a Core Data stack — one persistent store, one persistent store coordinator, and one managed object context — to build the example app. This setup is great for many simple persistency needs. If you can get away with it, use it, as it will save you from having to deal with the inherent complexities of concurrency.

In the previous chapter about syncing, we expanded this simple stack to use two managed object contexts — one on the main thread and one in the background — both connected to the same persistent store coordinator. This is the simplest and most battle-tested way to use Core Data concurrently. Unless you have very specific needs, it's probably the best setup for using multiple managed object contexts.

In this chapter, we will go into more detail about both this and other concurrent setups. And in the next chapter, we will then discuss some of the pitfalls related to using Core Data with multiple managed object contexts. But first, let's take a step back and revisit Core Data's concurrency model from the ground up.

Core Data and Concurrency

If you're not familiar with the concept of concurrency in general and dispatch queues specifically, we recommend you first read up on those concepts before progressing further in this chapter. Two good resources to start with are Apple's Concurrency Programming Guide and the objc.io issue from July 2013, which covers concurrent programming.

Core Data has a straightforward concurrency model: the managed object context and its managed objects **must** be accessed only from the context's queue. Everything below the context — i.e. the persistent store coordinator, the persistent store, and SQLite — is thread-safe and can be shared between multiple contexts.

When you initialize an NSManagedObjectContext instance, you already specify the concurrency type with the **init**(concurrencyType:) initializer. The first option, .MainQueueConcurrencyType, is what we used in part one of the book,

and it ties the context to the main queue. The second option,
.PrivateQueueConcurrencyType, ties the context to a private background
queue, which Core Data manages for you.

If you take only one thing away from this chapter, it should be this: **always**
dispatch onto the context's queue by calling performBlock(_:) before accessing
the context or the managed objects registered with it. This is the most
important rule for staying out of concurrency trouble.

Once you start working on multiple contexts, you'll want to reconcile the
changes at some point. This is done by observing one context's did-save
notification (see the chapter about changing and saving data for more details),
dispatching onto the other context's queue, and calling
mergeChangesFromContextDidSaveNotification(_:) to merge the changes
contained in the notification's userInfo dictionary:

```
let nc = NSNotificationCenter.defaultCenter()
token = nc.addObserverForName(
    NSManagedObjectContextDidSaveNotification, object: sourceContext,
    queue: nil) { note in
    targetContext.performBlock {
        targetContext.mergeChangesFromContextDidSaveNotification(note)
    }
}
```

Merging a did-save notification into a context will refresh the registered
objects that have been changed, remove the ones that have been deleted, and
fault in the ones that have been newly inserted. Then the context you're
merging into will send its own objects-did-change notification containing all
the changes to the context's objects:

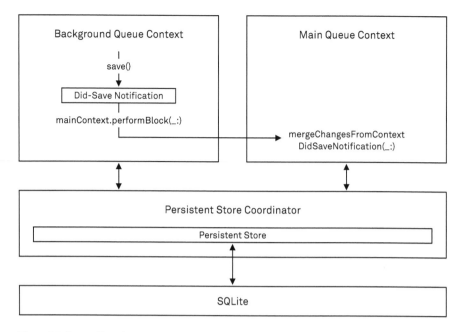

Figure 8.1: Reconciling changes between multiple contexts by merging their did-save notifications

This is the second most important message of this chapter that will keep you out of concurrency trouble: **totally separate** the work you do on different contexts, and exchange information between them **only** through the merging of their did-save notifications — avoid wild dispatching between contexts like the plague.

The above message might be a bit too strong insofar as there are use cases where you might want to pass objects from one context to another, e.g. when doing a complicated search in the background. Nevertheless, it's a good rule of thumb, and everything else should be a rare exception. For example, our sample app, with its syncing component, functions exactly in this way: all the syncing code works exclusively on its own managed object context, while the UI uses a separate managed object context. They only communicate with each other by merging the context-did-save notification.

Passing Objects Between Contexts

If you have to exchange objects between multiple contexts in a way other than by merging did-save notifications, you must use the indirect route: pass the object ID to the other context's queue using performBlock(_:), and re-instantiate the object there using the objectWithID(_:) API. For example:

```swift
func finishedBackgroundOperation(objects: [NSManagedObject]) {
    let ids = objects.map { $0.objectID }
    mainContext.performBlock {
        let results = ids.map(mainContext.objectWithID)
        // ... results can now be used on the main queue
    }
}
```

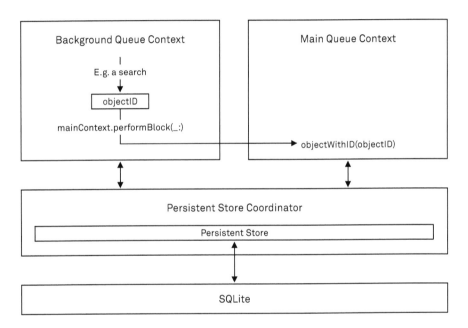

Figure 8.2: Handing a managed object from one context to another by passing its object ID

While it's technically correct that you should only pass the object IDs to another context and re-instantiate the object there, you can use a technique that will guarantee to keep the objects' row cache entries alive. This is useful because the target context can fulfill the object faults much quicker if the data is still in the row cache, compared to having to fetch it from SQLite.

You can achieve this by passing the objects themselves to the target context and extracting their IDs on the target context's queue. However, it's your responsibility to be very strict with this pattern — you *must not* use the objects in any way other than extracting their object IDs:

```
func finishedBackgroundOperation(objects: [NSManagedObject]) {
    mainContext.performBlock {
        let results = objects.map { mainContext.objectWithID($0.objectID) }
        // ... results can now be used on the main queue
    }
}
```

In case the object ID is coming from a context connected to a different persistent store coordinator, you first have to reconstruct the object ID for the current stack from its URIRepresentation. The coordinator provides the managedObjectIDForURIRepresentation(_:) API for this purpose:

```
func finishedBackgroundOperation(objects: [NSManagedObject]) {
    let ids = objects.map { $0.objectID }
    separatePSCContext.performBlock {
        let results = ids.map {
            (sourceID: NSManagedObjectID) -> NSManagedObject in
            let uri = sourceID.URIRepresentation()
            let psc = separatePSCContext.persistentStoreCoordinator!
            let targetID = psc.managedObjectIDForURIRepresentation(uri)!
            return separatePSCContext.objectWithID(targetID)
        }
        // ... results can now be used on the main queue
    }
}
```

(We're using force unwrapping in this snippet for brevity. You should always make your intent explicit using **guard** statements.) Note that in this case, there is no need to keep a reference to the objects themselves in order to keep their row cache entries alive; since the contexts don't share the same persistent store coordinator, they don't share a common row cache:

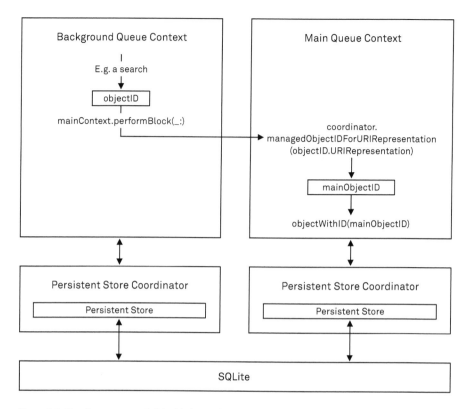

Figure 8.3: Handing a managed object between two contexts connected to different persistent store coordinators

Those are the basics of using Core Data correctly with multiple contexts. It's not so complicated in practice if you stick to the rules: strictly separate the work on multiple contexts, always dispatch onto the context's queue, and only pass object IDs between contexts.

Aside from these general rules, working concurrently with multiple contexts comes with complications — like conflicts and race conditions — that are inherent to concurrency itself. In the next chapter, we'll explain in detail how to handle those cases.

We already briefly mentioned how merging changes between contexts works. We will explain this more in depth now, before moving on to describe the advantages and disadvantages of several Core Data setups.

Merging Changes

Merging changes from one context into one (or multiple) other context(s) is relatively straightforward: we add an observer for Core Data's context-did-save notification. Within this observer code, we dispatch onto the target context's queue using performBlock(_:). We then call mergeChangesFromContextDidSaveNotification(_:) on this queue, passing in the notification as the argument.

During merging, Core Data will extract the object identifiers from the objects in the notification. It cannot use the objects themselves, since they must only be accessed on their own context's queue. Once the target context has a list of object IDs, it will process the changes in the following way:

→ Inserted objects will be faulted into the context.

   Note that these faults will be deallocated after the merging if nobody takes a strong reference to the inserted objects. You do have the chance to hold on to these objects when listening to the objects-did-change notification.

→ Updated objects that are registered in the context will be refreshed. All other updates will be ignored.

   If an updated object has pending changes in the target context, the changes will be merged property by property, with the changes in the target context winning out in the case of conflicts.

→ Deleted objects that are registered in the context will be removed. All other deletions will be ignored.

   If a deleted object has pending changes in the target context, it will be deleted regardless. It's your responsibility to react accordingly if you're currently using this object, like we did with the managed object change observer in the first chapter.

After merging is complete, processPendingChanges() gets called and posts an objects-did-change notification, as described in the chapter on changing and saving data. (Core Data may post multiple objects-did-change notifications for one merge operation – you should make no assumptions about that.) By observing this notification, you get the chance to react to any of the changes that were merged into the context. Keep in mind that changes in the did-save notification that didn't affect the target context (like updates of non-registered objects) will not be present in the did-change notification.

When passing a did-save notification from one context to another, the row cache entries of the objects involved are guaranteed to stay around via the same technique we described for passing objects between contexts above: the notification strongly references the source context and all objects affected by the save. Since we are using the notification object inside the closure passed to performBlock(_:), the notification itself will be strongly referenced. Therefore, at the time of the merge, the affected objects are still alive, and as we mentioned in the chapter on accessing data, this guarantees their row cache entries will stay around as well. This is an important detail, as it saves round trips to SQLite later on when the faults inserted by the merging process have to be fulfilled.

Core Data Stacks

Core Data allows for a lot of different setups: multiple contexts connected to one coordinator, multiple contexts chained behind each other, multiple coordinators, and multiple stores. There are literally endless possibilities, and each setup comes with its own set of tradeoffs. In this section, we'll describe the most common setups in detail and discuss which situations you might want to use them in.

Two Contexts, One Coordinator

This is the "classic" battle-tested setup to do Core Data work in the background: you create one main queue context, which you use for all UI-related work. Then you create a second private queue context, which you use for background work, like importing data from a web service. Both contexts share the same persistent store coordinator:

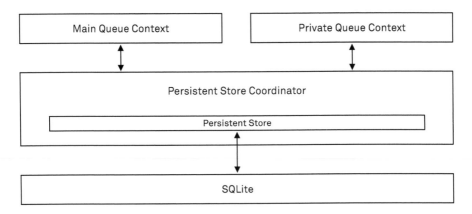

Figure 8.4: The "classic" setup for doing work in the background: two contexts connected to the same persistent store coordinator

This is the setup we used in the previous chapter about syncing in order to integrate our example app with a web service. It's our go-to setup for most concurrent Core Data tasks.

Advantages:

→ It's simple. Each context operates independently of the other. Changes are exchanged by merging the did-save notification.

→ You can do work on the background context, including fetch requests and saves, without blocking the main queue. (There is a gotcha to that, which we'll get to in a second.)

→ Both contexts share the same row cache in the coordinator layer. This avoids unnecessary round trips to SQLite. For example, when you create and save an object in one context, you don't have to refetch it from SQLite in the other context. The object fault can be fulfilled from the data that's already in the row cache.

→ You have fine-grained control over how conflicts are handled via each context's merge policy. We'll go into more detail about that in the next chapter.

Disadvantages:

→ You can have contention on the store coordinator level if you're doing a ton of work in the background.

Since both contexts share the same store coordinator, only one context can use it at a time. For example, if the background context is doing a really large import of data, executing many fetch and save requests, the main context may have to wait a bit if it has to fetch data from the store as well.

→ You can run into edge cases where you try to access an object in one context that has already been deleted by the other context.

This can happen when, for example, the main context holds a reference to a fault that the background context deletes. Then there is a short window of time after the deletion has been persisted but before the main context knows about this change. Accessing the fault at that moment will cause an exception. Core Data cannot fulfill the fault because the object doesn't exist anymore. We'll show you in the next chapter how to handle this.

Two Coordinators

In this setup, we create two independent stacks that only share the same underlying SQLite database. This alleviates the point of contention at the coordinator level that we described in the previous setup. Therefore, this approach might be a good option if you have to, for example, do very large data imports in the background. Apple has a sample project showing exactly this use case:

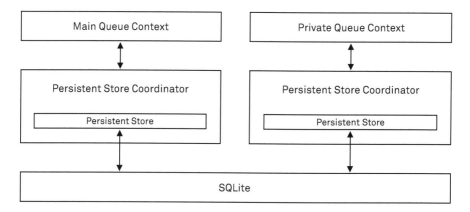

Figure 8.5: Maximum concurrency for heavy background work with two contexts connected to separate persistent store coordinators

However, performance is not the only reason you might use such a setup. If you want to access the same SQLite database from two different processes, you'll have the same situation. A common example of this is an application (on OS X) that uses a daemon. Both the main application and the daemon need to access the same data; as such, each has its own Core Data stack accessing the same SQLite database. On iOS, the same situation occurs when the SQLite database is located in a shared container and both the main app and an app extension access it.

This setup pushes the potential point of contention down the stack to the SQLite level. SQLite can handle a single write operation and multiple read operations at the same time, so you're much less likely to run into blocking issues. However, if you try to save data from both contexts at the same time, one will still have to wait for the other to finish.

Advantages:

→ Both stacks operate completely independent of one another. The only shared resource is the SQLite database. This gives you great concurrency for expensive background work.

Disadvantages:

→ The row cache is not shared between the contexts.

Since the row cache resides at the coordinator level, each stack manages its own cache. If you, for example, insert new objects in one context, the other context has to fetch the data for those objects from SQLite again. Similarly, if you update existing objects in one context, the other context has to refetch those objects from the persistent store to update the row cache in its coordinator.

Merging changes between contexts with distinct persistent store coordinators is no longer purely an in-memory operation, in contrast to the shared coordinator setup. It always involves a round trip to SQLite to retrieve the latest data.

→ Object IDs cannot be used across multiple coordinators. Instead, you have to fall back to an object ID's URIRepresentation.

Since the unique identifier of the persistent store is part of the object ID, an ID created in one stack cannot be used directly in another stack with a distinct coordinator. You have to use the coordinator's managedObjectIDForURIRepresentation(_:) API to convert the URI representation of one object ID from a different coordinator to a valid object ID for the current coordinator.

NSManagedObjectContext's APIs for merging changes — mergeChangesFromContextDidSaveNotification(_:), and the static method mergeChangesFromRemoteContextSave(_:intoContexts:) — take care of this automatically.

Setups with Nested Contexts

With iOS 5 and OS X 10.7, Core Data gained a new feature called *nested contexts*. Before, a managed object context always had to be connected directly to a persistent store coordinator. Now you can connect a context to another context instead.

In the next two sections, we'll first describe two good use cases for nested contexts. Afterward, we'll talk about the ways that nested contexts shouldn't be used and go into detail as to why that is.

Main Context as Child of a Private Context

One of the primary use cases for nested contexts is to enable background saves of large changes. With the traditional setup, your main (UI) context is directly connected to the persistent store. When you save a lot of changes in this context at once, the UI might be blocked for a moment. An example of this is a user pasting in a huge document from the clipboard, all of which has to be saved in one go.

Using nested contexts, you can reduce the amount of blocking work that has to be done on the main queue context by introducing a private queue context between the main context and the coordinator:

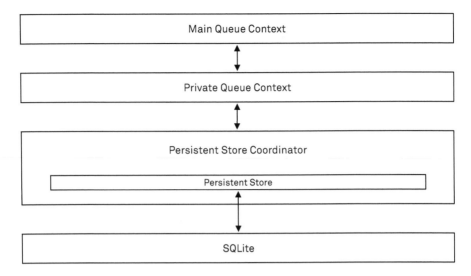

Figure 8.6: Deferred saving of large changes in the main context by using a private parent context

In this setup, saving the main context is purely an in-memory operation, since the changes only get pushed down to the parent context. The expensive part of the save involving I/O only happens when you save the private queue context itself. But since it's a private queue context, this will not flat out block your UI.

This is not a silver bullet; there's still the potential for contention. If you try to execute another save or fetch request from the main context while the private context is persisting the data, the main context will still have to wait. The private queue context needs to lock itself while it saves, effectively blocking the main queue context's access to the persistent store coordinator and the store.

Advantages:

→ Expensive I/O for saving large changesets from the UI context can be deferred to the parent background context.

→ It's straightforward to use in this basic configuration of one parent private context and one child main context.

Disadvantages:

→ If you want to extend this setup with additional child contexts or separate top-level contexts, there are all kinds of complications you should be aware of. We'll go into more detail about those below. Make sure that you actually have a performance problem with persisting data from the main queue context before using this setup, as it comes at a cost.

Child Contexts as Scratchpads

Another good use case for nested contexts is to use child contexts as throwaway scratchpads. You can attach another main queue context as a child to your main UI context and use it to make changes without affecting other parts of your application. Later you can decide if you actually want to persist or discard these changes.

A typical example of this is an edit dialog of a contacts application: you can make changes to the contact's properties or even modify or add related objects like addresses. If the user cancels the dialog, you can simply throw the child context away. If the user saves the changes, you save the child context to push the new data into the main context, and then save the main context itself.

The setup looks something like this:

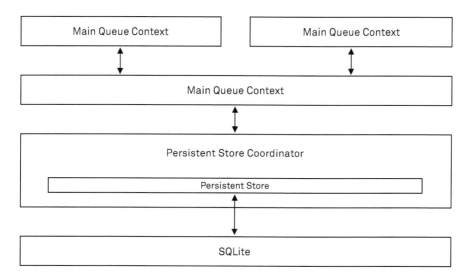

Figure 8.7: Using child contexts as discardable scratchpads

Advantages:

→ Changes can be accumulated in child contexts without affecting other parts of your app.

Disadvantages:

→ Saving a child context will push all changes to its parent context, *overriding* potential unsaved changes in the parent. It's your responsibility to make sure that this behavior works for your use case.

Keep in mind that this setup does nothing for you in terms of concurrency; it's simply a way of providing isolated scratchpads to make changes on.

When and Why You Shouldn't Use Nested Contexts

Using nested contexts in your app comes with an entire set of additional complexity. The good news is that you can ignore this added complexity if you continue to use Core Data as if nested contexts didn't exist. However, if you plan on using nested contexts, and especially using them beyond the two use cases we outlined above, you should be aware of the added complexity and pitfalls.

In this section, we'll first show an example of how nested contexts should not be used, and then we'll go into further detail about the unexpected behavior you can run into.

You'll often see nested contexts suggested as a way of performing background tasks on your data, basically as a replacement for the setup we outlined above, with two separate contexts and one coordinator. Such setups look something like this:

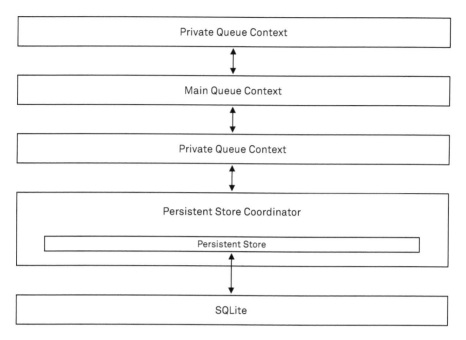

Figure 8.8: An example of a setup using nested contexts that we do *not* recommend

The idea is to use the last private queue context in the chain for background tasks. There are four main disadvantages to this approach:

→ Every fetch request you execute in the private child context will block the UI for the duration of the request. The same goes for fulfilling faults from the persistent store.

Since requests are synchronous (apart from asynchronous fetch requests), they will block all parent contexts between the originating context and the persistent store coordinator. Depending on the kind of work you do on the background context, you might get away with this. However, it goes against the goal of doing the background work in a way that has as little impact as possible on the UI.

→ When you save the private context, *all* changes are pushed down into the main context.

Without nested contexts, we'd merge a did-save notification into the main context to update it with the changes made in the private context. This process can ignore all changes made to objects that are not registered with the main context. In contrast, when saving the nested private context, the main context has to recreate all objects that have been changed, irrespective of whether or not they're relevant to the main context.

→ Every save has to go through the main queue context. You no longer have the option to save without pushing the changes to the main context.

With two separate contexts, you can decide to not merge every context-did-save notification immediately and to first finish all your background work and then notify your UI to refresh itself in a different way (e.g. by manually refreshing the whole UI at once). This can actually be a sensible design choice in many cases when you import a lot of data — particularly if you know that the newly imported data does not affect what the user is already seeing — because you don't constantly update the UI while the user tries to use your app.

→ You don't have fine-grained control over how conflicts get resolved when you save the private context.

When you save a context that's connected to a persistent store coordinator, you can handle conflicts via the context's merge policy. When saving a child context, the merge policy is ignored and the data in the parent context is simply overwritten.

To be fair, there's one thing that's potentially easier with this setup: the edge case we described in the first setup — one context trying to fulfill a fault for an object that has already been deleted, but before it knows about this deletion — does not happen in this configuration **if** you never merge changes from parent to child. However, that's a big *if*, and there are other ways to cleanly solve this problem without introducing both the disadvantages outlined above and the additional complexity we'll get to next.

Overall, we strongly discourage the use of nested setups like this. They fall short in terms of having background work impact the UI as little as possible, all while introducing new issues at the same time.

Independent of the specific setup outlined above, nested contexts in general come with a list of complications. Next, we're going to discuss a few of them so that you can make an informed decision as to whether or not to use them, when to use them, and what you need to watch out for.

Temporary and Permanent Object IDs

Object IDs, represented by NSManagedObjectID instances, are a central building block of Core Data. They uniquely identify objects within all managed object contexts of the same persistent store coordinator. At least, that was the case before nested contexts came along. Let's take a step back and revisit how object IDs work without nested contexts.

When you create a new object in a managed object context, the object will have a temporary ID. Temporary IDs can be distinguished from permanent IDs by checking the temporaryID flag on NSManagedObjectID. Once you successfully save the context, the temporary ID will be exchanged for a permanent one, which is assigned by the underlying SQLite store. From now on, you can use this object ID across all contexts connected to the same coordinator to uniquely identify the object's entry in the persistent store. The IDs of two objects representing the same data will compare equal. (And you can even use them across coordinators with a simple transformation step via their URIRepresentation.)

Unfortunately, the situation is somewhat different when you use nested contexts. Managed objects in child contexts will always keep their temporary IDs, even after saving the context. Only the objects in the root context, i.e. the context that's directly connected to the persistent store coordinator, will have permanent IDs after the context has been saved. So the IDs of objects representing the same data within the scope of one persistent store coordinator don't necessarily compare equal anymore.

You can use the temporary and permanent IDs of an object interchangeably to retrieve an object, but only in a certain scope: from the context you created the object in down to the root context, and any context that's a direct child of this root context. Outside of this scope, you have to use the permanent ID. If you instantiate an object beyond this scope with the temporary ID using objectWithID(_:), you'll get an instance of a non-existing object back (and you'll crash if you try to use it).

If you need to pass on temporary object IDs from a child context to a context outside of the scope where the temporary ID is valid, you first need to explicitly obtain the permanent ID. The context provides an API for that: obtainPermanentIDsForObjects(_:). If the object hasn't yet been persisted by the parent context(s), this call will cause a round trip to SQLite.

One last remark on object IDs: things go especially bad if you use the temporary ID in a context that's a child of the originating context. Here, using objectWithID(_:) will return two different objects, depending on whether or not you use the permanent or the temporary ID. In other words, this breaks Core Data's uniquing guarantee — you suddenly have two objects within one context representing the same data. If you modify both objects and try to save the changes, things will only get worse.

By now it should be clear what we mean when we say that nested contexts introduce *additional complexity*. We're not spelling all this out to make nested contexts look bad — as we mentioned above, they have valid use cases. We just want you to be aware of the pitfalls so that you can make an informed decision of whether or not they are an appropriate tool for the problem at hand.

Mixing Nested Contexts with Separate Contexts

A stack of nested parent-child contexts doesn't mix very well with other approaches of using multiple contexts. For example, you could try to combine parent-child contexts with another separate context to get the advantages of both setups: deferred background saves from the UI, and an independent context for imports. The setup could look like this:

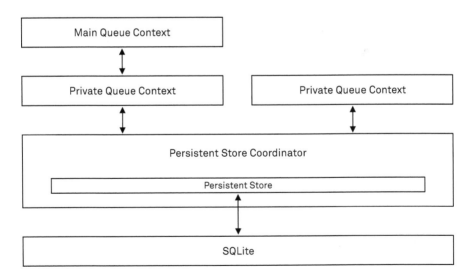

Figure 8.9: Mixing nested with parallel contexts is non-trivial

This sounds good on paper, but unfortunately it has a bunch of problems in reality. The first issue is that merging changes from the separate context into the main context no longer works as you might expect. For updated objects, merging a context-did-save notification will simply refresh those objects in the main context. But since the main context is a child of another context, the main context will try to get the new data from its parent, which will potentially still return the old data.

On iOS 9 and OS X 10.11, you can use the static mergeChangesFromRemoteContextSave(_:intoContexts:) method on NSManagedObjectContext to solve this problem. The second parameter should be an array of the nested contexts that should be updated. Note that this is a much more expensive operation than a normal did-save notification merge; therefore, it will have a greater impact on your UI.

On earlier versions, you'd have to solve this manually. For example, you could merge the save notification into the parent context *first*, and then merge it into the child context. (Since they operate on different queues, you'll have to make sure that those merges *really* run in sequence.) Another approach could be to manually refresh all updated objects in the parent context before merging the context-did-save notification into the child context.

An additional non-trivial issue is that, depending on your merge policy, the save of the parent context can now either fail or merge the new data with the data in the store. This could happen if the separate context has made changes in the persistent store to the same data that you're trying to save from the parent context. However, the main (child) context wouldn't know about the failed save or the merging of conflicted data. It's your responsibility to manually roll back the changes in the main context or to account for the results of conflict merging.

These problems are not insurmountable, but accounting for these edge cases makes your code more complex and harder to understand.

As a general rule, you should use the *simplest* stack you can get away with. It's much easier to reason about what's happening in your program if you cut down on complexity as much as you can.

In the next chapter, we will go through the complications of the complex setups that we mentioned throughout this chapter and discuss how to mitigate them.

Summary

Core Data offers great flexibility in setting up its stack according to your needs. Not all possible setups make sense though. In this chapter, we went over the most common variants:

1. A single (main queue) context if you don't have to do work that would block the UI.

2. Separate main queue and private queue contexts with one coordinator for most kinds of background work, such as syncing with a web service.

3. Main queue and private queue contexts with separate coordinators for heavy background work with the least possible effect on the UI.

4. A main queue context as child of a private queue context for deferred background saving of large amounts of changes from the UI.

5. Main queue contexts as children of the master main queue context as discardable scratchpads.

Takeaways

→ Use the simplest setup you can get away with.

→ Always dispatch onto a context's queue before accessing the context or its managed objects.

→ Separate the work you do on different contexts as much as possible, ideally with the context-did-save notifications as the only point of contact.

→ Only pass object IDs between contexts. You can pass the objects themselves to keep their row cache entries alive, but you must only access their objectID properties on a different context's queue.

→ Nested contexts add significant complexity. Ask yourself if they solve the problem you're facing better than a simpler setup.

Problems with Multiple Contexts

9

Once you start working with multiple managed object contexts at the same time, conflicts between the changes you make in those contexts can occur.

In part two, we mentioned conflicts during saving and how Core Data detects them with a two-step optimistic locking approach. In this chapter, we'll go into more detail about how to use the predefined merge policies to resolve such conflicts, as well as how to define a custom merge policy.

We'll also discuss how to avoid race conditions that can occur when deleting objects, as well as how you can enforce uniqueness requirements with multiple managed object contexts.

Save Conflicts

When you work with multiple managed object contexts at once, conflicts can occur when trying to save changes in different contexts. These contexts don't have to operate concurrently — conflicts can even occur between multiple main queue contexts.

We already mentioned snapshots in the chapter about changing and saving data. Snapshots are dictionaries of raw data that are associated with every managed object. They represent the last known persisted data for each object, including a version identifier used for optimistic locking: when you try to save changes, Core Data will compare those version identifiers between the different layers of the Core Data stack. This way, Core Data knows when the persisted data has changed, compared to the data in the managed object that should be saved. This is called a *save conflict*.

Conflicts can happen at two different points:

1. Between the snapshot and the data in the persistent store's row cache
2. Between the persistent store's row cache and the data in SQLite

The first type of conflict can happen when you have multiple contexts connected to the same persistent store coordinator. The second type of conflict can happen if you're working with multiple coordinators on the same persistent store.

In any case, the way these conflicts are handled is determined by the context's merge policy. Merge policies are represented by instances of the

NSMergePolicy class, and there are several predefined ones that cover the most common cases. The default merge policy is NSErrorMergePolicy, which does not attempt to resolve the conflicts, but instead throws an error, with the code NSManagedObjectMergeError containing detailed information about the conflicts.

To determine what exactly went wrong, you can inspect the value of the "conflictList" key in the error's userInfo dictionary, which is an array of NSMergeConflict objects.[1] Each of these objects has several properties containing the details of a particular conflict:

→ sourceObject is a reference to the managed object that caused that particular merge conflict.

→ objectSnapshot, cachedSnapshot, and persistedSnapshot are dictionaries containing the current snapshot data on multiple levels, i.e. the managed object, the persistent store coordinator, and the persistent store. Which one of these properties is non-**nil** depends on where the conflict actually occurred.

→ newVersionNumber and oldVersionNumber contain the version numbers of the conflicting datasets, e.g. the one in the row cache and the one in the persistent store. Version numbers are simply integers associated with each record in the database and are incremented on each change. This way, Core Data can determine whether or not a snapshot is out of date relative to another dataset.

When a conflict with the default NSErrorMergePolicy occurs, it is up to you to both resolve it in whatever manner is appropriate for your use case and resave any pending changes. If the conflict occurred between the row cache and SQLite, Core Data updates the row cache with the currently persisted values. This makes it possible to update the properties of a managed object with the values from store while maintaining unsaved changes: just call refreshObjects(_:mergeChanges:) with the last argument as **true**. Refreshing an object will not only update the data of the entity's attributes, but it will also update the object's optimistic locking version identifier.

---

1 At the time of writing, Apple's documentation of the default merge policy's error is out of date.

Predefined Merge Policies

Next to the default merge policy that simply throws an error, Core Data comes with four predefined policies that cover all important standard cases:

1. NSRollbackMergePolicy

   This policy simply discards the changes on objects that cause a conflict during the save. Objects that don't cause conflicts will still be saved normally.

2. NSOverwriteMergePolicy

   With this merge policy, *all* data in the persistent store will be replaced by the data in the objects you're trying to save. There's no merging occurring on an attribute-by-attribute basis — if there's a conflict, your in-memory changes will win, and all properties of those objects (not only the ones with pending changes) will be written to the store.

3. NSMergeByPropertyStoreTrumpMergePolicy

   As the first half of its name suggests, this merge policy actually merges conflicting changes within one object, attribute by attribute. If an attribute has been changed in the store but not in memory, then the store version will be used. If an attribute has been changed in memory but not in the store, the in-memory version will be persisted. However, if the attribute has been changed both in the store and in memory, the second half of this policy's name, StoreTrumpMergePolicy, indicates what will happen — changes in the persistent store will win.

4. NSMergeByPropertyObjectTrumpMergePolicy

   This policy operates similar to the previous one, but this time, the in-memory changes will win if an attribute has been changed both in the store and in memory.

All of these standard merge policies are defined as singleton objects and can be readily used by assigning them to the managed object context's mergePolicy property.

Which one (if any) of the predefined policies you should use depends entirely on your particular use case and what behavior makes most sense for the user.

Custom Merge Policies

Next to those predefined merge policies, you can also create custom ones by subclassing NSMergePolicy.

So far, we've used the object-trump policy for the background context, which communicates with the web service, and the store-trump policy for the UI context. This setup reflects a "the server is the truth" approach: imported data from the web service trumps conflicting changes that have been made from the UI context.

Now we'll create a custom merge policy that adds a detail on top of those default merge policies: Country and Continent both have an updatedAt property that's being used for sorting in the table view so that the regions with the latest updates will appear at the top. We want to merge this updatedAt property so that the most recent date wins.

When considering a custom merge policy, you should always build on top of an existing one. Choose the predefined merge policy that's closest to what you want and add your custom merging rules on top of that. This is exactly what we're going to do: we'll keep the store-trump and object-trump policies for the UI and the syncing context, respectively, but we'll add our custom behavior on top of them.

We start by implementing our own required initializer to encapsulate the standard merge type we're building on internally:

```swift
public class MoodyMergePolicy: NSMergePolicy {
    public enum MergeMode {
        case Remote
        case Local

        private var mergeType: NSMergePolicyType {
            switch self {
            case .Remote: return .MergeByPropertyObjectTrumpMergePolicyType
            case .Local: return .MergeByPropertyStoreTrumpMergePolicyType
            }
        }
    }

    required public init(mode: MergeMode) {
        super.init(mergeType: mode.mergeType)
    }
```

```
    // ...
}
```

To implement the custom merging logic, we override
resolveOptimisticLockingVersionConflicts(_:) (this method has existed since
iOS 9 / OS X 10.11; in earlier versions you'd have to overwrite
resolveConflicts(_:)):

```
public class MoodyMergePolicy: NSMergePolicy {
    // ...
    override public func resolveOptimisticLockingVersionConflicts(
        list : [NSMergeConflict]) throws
    {
        var regionsAndLatestDates: [(UpdateTimestampable, NSDate)] = []
        for (c, r) in list .conflictsAndObjectsWithType(UpdateTimestampable) {
            regionsAndLatestDates.append((r, c.newestUpdatedAt))
        }

        try super.resolveOptimisticLockingVersionConflicts(list)

        for (var region, date) in regionsAndLatestDates {
            region.updatedAt = date
        }
    }
}
```

In this method, we first iterate over all conflicts where the involved managed
object is of type UpdateTimestampable (see the sample code[2] for the definition
of the conflictsAndObjectsWithType(_:) helper). This is a simple protocol
containing the updatedAt property that both Country and Continent adopt.
During this iteration, we remember the object-date tuples, extracting the
newest updatedAt values from the NSMergeConflict instances. For that, we use
the following helper:

```
extension NSMergeConflict {
    var newestUpdatedAt: NSDate {
        guard let o = sourceObject as? UpdateTimestampable else {
            fatalError("must be UpdateTimestampable")
        }
        let key = UpdateTimestampKey
        let zeroDate = NSDate(timeIntervalSince1970: 0)
```

2 https://github.com/objcio/core-data/blob/master/Moody/MoodyModel/MoodyMergePolicy.swift

```
        let objectDate = objectSnapshot?[key] as? NSDate ?? zeroDate
        let cachedDate = cachedSnapshot?[key] as? NSDate ?? zeroDate
        let persistedDate = persistedSnapshot?[key] as? NSDate ?? zeroDate
        return max(o.updatedAt, max(objectDate,
            max(cachedDate, persistedDate)))
    }
}
```

Merge conflict instances have a sourceObject property containing the managed object that caused the conflict. Furthermore, they have three properties — objectSnapshot, cachedSnapshot, and persistedSnapshot — containing the object's snapshots on the context, the row cache, and the SQLite level. We simply extract the newest date value from all these sources and return it.

After we've extracted the update dates that we want to win out in the end, we call the superclass's implementation of resolveOptimisticLockingVersionConflicts(_:). This ensures that all existing conflicts will first be resolved with the predefined policy type that has been specified at the initialization of the MoodyMergePolicy instance. Afterward, we apply our previously stored date values to the conflicted Country and Continent objects.

Other cases where we need to handle conflict resolution ourselves are the denormalized attributes numberOfMoods and numberOfCountries, which we introduced in the chapter about performance. Here, the conflict resolution is a bit more complicated, since we can't just pick one of the conflicting values. In the case of the Country class, we have to get the correct number of moods by refreshing the country object and accessing the moods relationship:

```
public class MoodyMergePolicy: NSMergePolicy {
    // ...
    func resolveCountryConflicts(conflicts: [NSMergeConflict]) {
        for country in conflicts.conflictedObjectsWithType(Country) {
            country.refresh()
            country.numberOfMoods = Int64(country.moods.count)
        }
    }
}
```

For continents, we have to go one step further and refetch the number of moods from SQLite:

```
public class MoodyMergePolicy: NSMergePolicy {
    // ...
    func resolveContinentConflicts(conflicts: [NSMergeConflict]) {
        for continent in conflicts.conflictedObjectsWithType(Continent) {
            continent.refresh()
            continent.numberOfCountries = Int64(continent.countries.count)
            guard let ctx = continent.managedObjectContext else { continue }
            let count = Mood.countInContext(ctx) { request in
                request.predicate = Mood.predicateWithFormat("country IN %@",
                    args: continent.countries)
            }
            continent.numberOfMoods = Int64(count)
        }
    }
}
```

Custom merge policies are difficult to test just by using your app, since you have to get your Core Data stack into a specific state to trigger the right code path in the merge policy. It's much easier to write automated tests for those cases. You can find the tests for the policies outlined above in the sample code[3].

To use our custom merge policy, we have to set it on both managed object contexts:

```
public func createMoodyMainContext() -> NSManagedObjectContext {
    // ...
    context.mergePolicy = MoodyMergePolicy(mode: .Local)
    // ...
}

public final class SyncCoordinator {
    public init (
        mainManagedObjectContext mainMOC: NSManagedObjectContext)
    {
        // ...
        syncManagedObjectContext.mergePolicy =
            MoodyMergePolicy(mode: .Remote)
        // ...
    }
}
```

3 https://github.com/objcio/core-data/blob/master/Moody/MoodyModelTests/MoodyMergePolicyTests.swift

Deleting Objects

Once you work with two or more contexts concurrently, you may have to be careful how you handle object deletions.

In most setups with more than one context, deletions can trigger a crash: if in one context there's an object that's a fault, and the corresponding object gets deleted in another context, the first context can no longer fulfill its fault. If the fault is triggered, it will lead to a runtime exception because the object is referencing data that does not exist.

When a context deletes an object, all other contexts must merge the deleting context's changes. Once the changes have been merged, any objects that were deleted in the original context will also be marked as deleted in the other contexts, and accessing them will no longer cause a crash. However, if a merging context uses a different queue than the original context, there is still a window where the merging context could be accessing the fault before it has merged the changes:

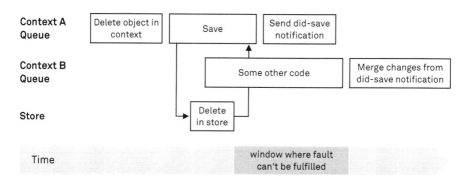

Figure 9.1: Deleting an object in one context creates a window of time where accessing the same object on a different queue can cause a crash

This problem does not happen if there's only one context or if all contexts are main queue contexts. In those situations, all contexts are on the same queue, and as long as contexts merge changes into one another, faults for deleted objects will also be marked as deleted synchronously.

If the code needs to use multiple contexts operating on different queues, there are two ways to solve this problem.

As of iOS 9 and OS X 10.11, there's a property called shouldDeleteInaccessibleFaults that we can set on NSManagedObjectContext. If it is set and the context tries to fulfill a fault that no longer has data in the store, the object will simply be marked as deleted.

It is a very simple solution, but this sledgehammer approach comes with a few downsides to be aware of: any relationships on a deleted object will be **nil** after such an event, and attributes will either be zero or **nil**, depending on their attribute types. This only works if all attributes are modeled as optional. If any of the object's attributes are represented by non-optional types in the managed object subclass, accessing one of these properties will crash at runtime if the object has been deleted. Furthermore, when shouldDeleteInaccessibleFaults is enabled, Core Data cannot enforce non-optional validation rules on attributes any longer.

If these restrictions are fine for your app, then setting shouldDeleteInaccessibleFaults is the easiest solution. Just be sure to check how each attribute and relationship behaves and if that is reflected in the way your model class exposes those attributes and relationships as optional or non-optional.

Two-Step Deletion

Another strategy for the problem is called two-step deletion, and it has the benefit of also working on systems earlier than iOS 9 and OS X 10.11. Rather than deleting objects outright, we first mark them as "in progress of being deleted." That update is then merged into all contexts. At this point, all contexts *must* release any references to objects that are marked with this attribute. Once this change has been merged and all contexts have released their references to these objects, the original context then deletes the objects at a convenient time.

A relatively straightforward implementation of this approach is to add an optional markedForDeletionDate attribute to your entities and a markForLocalDeletion() method to your managed object subclasses, which will set this attribute. We'll define this functionality in the DelayedDeletable protocol, which will be adopted by all our managed object subclasses:

```
public protocol DelayedDeletable: class {
    var markedForDeletionDate: NSDate? { get set }
    func markForLocalDeletion()
}
```

Calling the markForLocalDeletion() method sets the deletion to the current date and time:

```
extension DelayedDeletable where Self: ManagedObject {
    public func markForLocalDeletion() {
        guard fault || markedForDeletionDate == nil else { return }
        markedForDeletionDate = NSDate()
    }
}
```

By default, this markedForDeletionDate value is **nil**, and the UI filters out objects where this value is set. We can achieve this very easily by modifying the default predicate defined on ManagedObjectType, which is being used by all fetch requests from the UI.

First we expose a predicate property from the DelayedDeletable protocol to filter for objects that haven't been deleted:

```
extension DelayedDeletable {
    public static var notMarkedForLocalDeletionPredicate: NSPredicate {
        return NSPredicate(format: "%K == NULL", MarkedForDeletionDateKey)
    }
}
```

Then we return this predicate as the default predicate — for example, here in Country's ManagedObjectType extension:

```
extension Country: ManagedObjectType {
    // ...
    public static var defaultPredicate: NSPredicate {
        return notMarkedForLocalDeletionPredicate
    }
}
```

With this solution, the app can execute a fetch request at convenient times for objects where the markedForDeletionDate property is not **nil** and the date lies in the past more than a certain amount of time (for example, two minutes). Any matching objects will then be permanently deleted from the database. One possibility is to perform this step when the app enters the background.

On iOS 9 and OS X 10.11, this can be done very efficiently using a batch delete. We know at this point that nobody is holding a reference to these objects anymore, so we don't have to worry about updating the managed object contexts after the batch operation, as described in the section about batch updates:

```
extension ManagedObjectType where Self: ManagedObject {
    private static func batchDeleteObjectsMarkedForLocalDeletionInContext(
        managedObjectContext: NSManagedObjectContext)
    {
        let fetchRequest = NSFetchRequest(entityName: entityName)
        let cutoff = NSDate(timeIntervalSinceNow:
            -DeletionAgeBeforePermanentlyDeletingObjects)
        fetchRequest.predicate = NSPredicate(
            format: "%K < %@", MarkedForDeletionDateKey, cutoff)
        let batchRequest = NSBatchDeleteRequest(
            fetchRequest: fetchRequest)
        batchRequest.resultType = .ResultTypeStatusOnly
        try! managedObjectContext.executeRequest(batchRequest)
    }
}
```

On earlier OS versions, for the objects to be deleted you'll have to perform a regular fetch request, delete the objects, and then save the context again.

Delete Propagation

Once you adopt a two-step deletion approach, naturally Core Data's relationship delete rules will not take effect as long as an object is only *marked* for deletion but not actually deleted. If you need an object marked for deletion to be removed from a relationship, you have to do this manually.

We have such a case in our example app: in the relationships chapter, we implemented a custom delete rule in prepareForDeletion() to delete Country objects that don't reference Mood objects any longer, along with Continent objects that don't reference Country objects any longer. With two-step deletion, prepareForDeletion() will not be called until the object is permanently deleted.

In order to restore this functionality, we'll hook into the managed object's willSave() method. For example, in the Country, we set the continent relationship to nil if the country has been marked for deletion:

```
public override func willSave() {
    // ...
    if changedForDelayedDeletion {
        removeFromContinent()
```

```
    }
}
```

The changedForDelayedDeletion property is implemented as an extension on the DelayedDeletable protocol, checking whether or not the managed object's markedForDeletionDate property has unsaved changes:

```
extension DelayedDeletable where Self: ManagedObject {
    public var changedForDelayedDeletion: Bool {
        return changedValues()[MarkedForDeletionDateKey] as? NSDate != nil
    }
}
```

Uniqueness Constraints

Often you have to make sure that an object with a specific identifier or any other kind of uniquely identifying information only exists once in your store. An example of this is the *Country* entity in the *Moody* app. Each country is identified by its numeric country code, and we should never be in a state where two country records exist in SQLite with the same country code.

We have to worry about this requirement as soon as we start creating Country objects in more than one managed object context. For example, the following could happen: we create the country object for France on the main context by snapping a new mood in Paris, while at the same time, a mood taken in France by somebody else gets pushed to us from the server. Now the background sync context gets saved (and thus the country object for France persisted), and a little bit later we save the main context as well. Voilà, we have created two entries for France in SQLite.

One solution to this problem is to only ever insert new objects with uniqueness requirements in one managed object context. In fact, that's the only solution you can take if you have to support versions prior to iOS 9 and OS X 10.11.

In iOS 9 and OS X 10.11, Core Data gained a new feature called *uniqueness constraints*. This lets us specify these uniqueness requirements per entity. You can specify the constraints in code on NSEntityDescription or in the data model inspector.

Creating a uniqueness constraint containing the *numericISO3166Code* attribute on the *GeographicRegion* entity will enforce the uniqueness of Country and Continent objects on two different levels when we save changes:[4]

1. Multiple objects within one managed object context must satisfy the constraint when the context is saved.

2. The data in the persistent store in conjunction with the object being saved must satisfy the constraint.

This process might remind you of the two-step optimistic locking approach used to detect conflicts during saving. In fact, uniqueness constraint conflicts are reported and resolved via the same mechanism as optimistic locking conflicts: the context's merge policy.

As with optimistic locking conflicts, in the case of uniqueness constraint conflicts, the save operation will throw an error if you don't set a merge policy on the saving context. You can get the details of what went wrong by inspecting the NSConstraintConflict objects under the "conflictList" key in the error's userInfo dictionary.

If you use one of the predefined merge policies described above, it will also resolve uniqueness constraint conflicts for you. All of the predefined policies will resolve uniqueness constraint conflicts between multiple objects within the context by picking one of those objects. However, when it comes to resolving constraint conflicts between an object and the persisted state, their behavior differs:

1. NSRollbackMergePolicy

   The persisted state always wins, and the conflicting changes in the context are rolled back.

2. NSOverwriteMergePolicy

   The changes in the context win over the persisted state. In this case, the object that got displaced by the changes will be deleted.

3. NSMergeByPropertyStoreTrumpMergePolicy

   This policy behaves like NSRollbackMergePolicy.

4 There's a bug at the time of writing (rdar://22753815) that prevents us from creating a uniqueness constraint on a single integer attribute. We include a second dummy Int16 attribute in the constraint to work around this issue.

4. NSMergeByPropertyObjectTrumpMergePolicy

The persisted object will stay around, and the conflicting unsaved change will be rolled back. However, changed properties of the unsaved object will be merged into the persisted object.

One common factor between all of these merge policies is that objects might get deleted during saving if they are involved in a uniqueness constraint conflict. If that happens, you have to make sure to cut any references you might hold to these objects. Such changes are reported in the objects-did-change notification. That's another point where consequently taking a reactive approach to handling changes pays off: an object that gets deleted because of a uniqueness constraint conflict gets handled in the same way as, for example, an object that gets deleted because of a change on the server.

You can also fine-tune the handling of uniqueness constraint conflicts in a custom NSMergePolicy subclass. For example, you might have specific criteria for the conflicting objects within the context that you want to win out over the others. You can implement such rules by overriding resolveConstraintConflicts(_:).

Summary

As soon as you work with multiple, possibly concurrent contexts, you have to think about setting the right merge policies on your contexts. If the predefined merge policies don't work for you, pick the one that is closest to what you want and build a custom NSMergePolicy subclass on top of that.

When using multiple managed object contexts concurrently, you also have to handle race conditions when deleting objects. Both iOS 9 and OS X 10.11 have a convenient solution for this problem in the form of the context's shouldDeleteInaccessibleFaults property. However, this convenience comes with tradeoffs. Alternatively, you can implement robust deletion using a two-step deletion process.

Lastly, you also have to think about whether or not you need to enforce uniqueness requirements on your objects. If so, and if you have to support versions prior to iOS 9 and OS X 10.11, you have to limit writing operations of the entity that has uniqueness requirements to one managed object context. If you don't have to support older versions, use Core Data's new uniqueness constraints.

Part 4
Advanced
Topics

Predicates

10

A predicate encapsulates criteria that an object either matches or doesn't. For example: the question or criteria "Is this person older than 32?" can be encoded into a predicate. We can then use this predicate to check if a *Person* object matches this criteria.

At the core of the NSPredicate class is the evaluateWithObject(_:) method, which takes an object and returns a boolean. Predicates have a special role in Core Data. Core Data can transform predicates into an SQL WHERE clause and hence use SQLite to efficiently evaluate the predicate against objects in the database without having to create objects in memory.

We use predicates to match a specific object or to filter a collection of objects to a smaller subset. Either way, it is worth noting that we can use predicates both as part of a fetch request and directly on objects with the evaluateWithObject(_:) method.

In this chapter, we will walk you through both simple predicates and more complex examples. The discussion in this chapter focuses on predicates used with Core Data. Predicates can also be used independently of Core Data, but we won't be going into details about that here.

You can find an accompanying playground[1] to this chapter on GitHub.

A Simple Example

The simplest predicate is one that checks for equality and inequality on numeric fields. If our *Person* entity has a 16-bit integer field called *age*, we can create a predicate to match objects where age is 32:

```
let predicate = NSPredicate(format: "age == 32")
```

While this works, we highly recommend not hardcoding attribute keys into predicate formats. It makes it very difficult to later change them or track down typos. Instead, we recommend defining a string-backed enum with each case corresponding to a key:

```
public class Person: ManagedObject {
    public enum Keys: String {
        case givenName
```

1 https://github.com/objcio/core-data

```
        case familyName
        case age
        //  ...
    }

    @NSManaged public var givenName: String
    @NSManaged public var familyName: String
    @NSManaged public var age: Int16
    //  ...
}
```

Using the above, we can build predicates, like so:

```
let predicate = NSPredicate(format: "%K == 32", Person.Keys.age.rawValue)
```

The %K format specifier is specific to NSPredicate and is intended for keys only.

Similarly, we can build other predicates for the age property:

```
let predicateA = NSPredicate(format: "%K <= 30", Person.Keys.age.rawValue)
let predicateB = NSPredicate(format: "%K > 30", Person.Keys.age.rawValue)
let predicateC = NSPredicate(format: "%K != 24", Person.Keys.age.rawValue)
```

Before we move on, we'll take a quick look at how we can use predicates.

Using Predicates

Fetch requests have an optional predicate property. But we can also evaluate a predicate directly by using evaluateWithObject(_:).

To do so, we simply pass the object that we want to evaluate to this method:

```
let predicate = NSPredicate(format: "age == 32")
if predicate.evaluateWithObject(person) {
    print("\(person.name) is 32 years old")
} else {
    print("\(person.name) is younger or older than 32 years")
}
```

To limit the result of a fetch request to objects matching a given predicate, we set the predicate on the fetch request:

```
let request = NSFetchRequest(entityName: Person.entityName)
request.fetchLimit = 1
request.predicate = NSPredicate(format: "age == 32")
let result = try! moc.executeFetchRequest(request) as! [Person]
if let person = result.first {
    print("\(person.name) is \(person.age) years old")
}
```

Creating Predicates in Code

It is worth pointing out that we can also construct predicates in code, although in practice, this is rarely used. Most of the time, we initialize predicates with a format string as we have seen above:

```
let predicate = NSPredicate(format: "%K < %ld", Person.Keys.age.rawValue, 32)
```

This is a *comparison predicate*. It has a left expression, the key path age; a right expression, the constant 32; and a comparison operator, <. We can build this kind of predicate using the NSComparisonPredicate class:

```
let predicate = NSComparisonPredicate(
    leftExpression: NSExpression(forKeyPath: Person.Keys.age.rawValue),
    rightExpression: NSExpression(forConstantValue: 32),
    modifier: .DirectPredicateModifier,
    type: NSPredicateOperatorType.EqualToPredicateOperatorType,
    options: [])
```

This is extremely verbose. But it gives us a lot of flexibility, which can be useful if we need to build predicates in a dynamic way. We could replace the key, constant, or comparison type at runtime.

The predicateFormat property on NSPredicate can be useful for debugging predicates that have been created in code. It returns the format string that would have generated the same predicate.

In addition to comparison predicates, there are also *compound predicates*. We'll talk more about those below.

Format Strings

Most of the time, it is easier to write and read predicates based on format strings.

As we mentioned at the beginning of this chapter, it is good practice not to hardcode any attribute names (i.e. *keys*) in the format string, but instead use the %K format specifier ("K" for key). Likewise, we can use the %ld format specifier for Int values:

```
let a: Int = 25
let predicate = NSPredicate(format: "%K == %ld", Person.Keys.age.rawValue, a)
```

For Double floating-point values, we should use the %la specifier. Meanwhile, for Float, we should use %a:

```
let a: Double = 25.6789012345679
let predicate = NSPredicate(format: "%K >= %la", Person.Keys.age.rawValue, a)
```

```
let a: Float = 25.67891
let predicate = NSPredicate(format: "%K <= %a", Person.Keys.age.rawValue, a)
```

And for NSDate or NSNumber instances (both of which are subclasses of NSObject), we have to use the %@ format specifier:

```
let day = NSDateComponents()
day.hour = -1
let date = NSCalendar.currentCalendar().dateByAddingComponents(
    day, toDate: NSDate(), options: .WrapComponents) ?? NSDate()
let predicate = NSPredicate(format: "%K < %@",
    Person.Keys.modificationDate.rawValue, date)
```

```
let age = NSNumber(integer: 25)
let predicate = NSPredicate(format: "%K == %@", Person.Keys.age.rawValue, age)
```

Be sure to check Apple's Predicate Format String Syntax document for full details on the syntax.

Comparison

There are several simple comparisons we can do with a predicate: the equal operator ==; inequality operators <, >, <=, and >=; and the *not equal* operator

!=. Some of these have alternate versions: =, =<, =>, and <>. All of these work with the above format specifiers.

We can check if a value is in a closed interval with a BETWEEN predicate such as 1 BETWEEN { 0 , 33 }. To create it, we use the %@ format specifier and pass an array with two values: the start and end of the closed interval. The predicate will match values equal to the start or end value, as well as values in between these values. Matching intervals works both for numeric ranges and ranges of dates.

We can use this to match *Person* entities that are 23 years or older, but no older than 28 years:

```
let predicate = NSPredicate(format: "%K BETWEEN %@",
    Person.Keys.age.rawValue, [23, 28]).predicateFormat
let predicate = NSPredicate(format: "%K BETWEEN {%ld, %ld}",
    Person.Keys.age.rawValue, 23, 28).predicateFormat
```

If we want to check if a value is one of multiple specific values, we can use the IN operator and pass an array or a set of the values we want to match:

```
let primeNumbers = [13, 17, 19, 23, 29, 31, 37, 41, 43, 47]
let predicate = NSPredicate(format: "%K IN %@",
    Person.Keys.age.rawValue, primeNumbers)
```

Optional Values

Core Data attributes can be made optional. However, optional attributes can behave counterintuitively in conjunction with predicates on fetch requests.

If the *Person* entity has an optional attribute called carsOwnedCount, we can set this attribute to either **nil** or an integer value. Consider the following:

```
let pA = NSPredicate(format: "%K == 1",
    Person.Keys.carsOwnedCount.rawValue)
let pB = NSPredicate(format: "%K >= 1",
    Person.Keys.carsOwnedCount.rawValue)
let pC = NSPredicate(format: "%K == nil",
    Person.Keys.carsOwnedCount.rawValue)
```

As expected, the predicates will match objects where carsOwnedCount is 1, 1 or larger, or **nil**, respectively. This works both when using these predicates on a fetch request and when using them with evaluateWithObject(_:).

However, consider this:

```
let pD = NSPredicate(format: "%K != 2",
    Person.Keys.carsOwnedCount.rawValue)
```

If we use the predicate to match objects where carsOwnedCount is not equal to 2, the meaning is not identical when using it with a fetch request and with evaluateWithObject(_:). When using it with a fetch request, SQLite will only return objects where carsOwnedCount is not 2 and is not **nil**. On the other hand, evaluateWithObject(_:) will return objects with a carsOwnedCount attribute of **nil**.

For that reason, it is important to add an explicit %K != **nil** to predicates when using *not equal* on optional attributes:

```
let pE = NSPredicate(format: "%K != 2 AND %K != nil",
    Person.Keys.carsOwnedCount.rawValue,
    Person.Keys.carsOwnedCount.rawValue)
```

This predicate will have the same behavior when used both with a fetch request and with evaluateWithObject(_:). When using optional values, the best approach is to always combine predicates with a check for either AND %K != **nil** or OR %K == **nil**, in order to be very explicit about what the predicate is supposed to match.

Dates

A date attribute on an object is represented as an NSDate instance. As one would expect, the inequality operators < and > will match dates that are either before or after a given date.

If our objects have a date attribute called modificationDate, we can use this to, for example, find objects that have a modification date older than one day:

```
let date = NSCalendar.currentCalendar().dateByAddingUnit(
    .Day, value: -1, toDate: NSDate(),
    options: .WrapComponents) ?? NSDate()
let predicate = NSPredicate(format: "%K < %@",
    Person.Keys.modificationDate.rawValue, date)
```

Internally, the NSDate class is a wrapper around a double-precision floating-point value that represents the time in seconds relative to the absolute reference date — 00:00:00 UTC on 1 January 2001. This double-precision floating-point value is what Core Data stores in the SQLite database, and predicates are evaluated based on it.

That is why equality comparisons based on dates will only match if the floating-point values match exactly. Hence, it is often better to check if dates are within a range:

```
let predicate = NSPredicate(format: "%K BETWEEN {%@, %@}",
    Person.Keys.modificationDate.rawValue, startDate, endDate)
```

Combining Predicates

We can combine multiple, simpler predicates with the logical operators AND, OR, and NOT. In this way, we can create more complex predicates:

```
let predicateA = NSPredicate(format: "%K >= 30 AND %K < 32",
    Person.Keys.age.rawValue, Person.Keys.age.rawValue)
let predicateB = NSPredicate(format: "%K == 30 OR %K == 31",
    Person.Keys.age.rawValue, Person.Keys.age.rawValue)
let predicateC = NSPredicate(format: "NOT %K == 24",
    Person.Keys.age.rawValue)
```

Often, we want to build these from existing predicates. We might, for example, have the following predicates, isRecentlyModifiedPredicate and isMayorPredicate, defined on Person:

```
extension Person {
    static var isRecentlyModifiedPredicate: NSPredicate {
        let date = NSCalendar.currentCalendar().dateByAddingUnit(
            .Day, value: -1, toDate: NSDate(),
            options: .WrapComponents) ?? NSDate()
        return NSPredicate(format: "%K < %@",
            Person.Keys.modificationDate.rawValue, date)
    }
    static var isMayorPredicate: NSPredicate {
        return NSPredicate(format: "%K != nil", Person.Keys.mayorOf.rawValue)
    }
}
```

If we want to build a predicate for "is mayor and is recently modified," we don't want to copy the existing logic. Instead, we'd like to combine the existing predicates. We can do this using an NSCompoundPredicate, which supports all three logical operators — AND, OR, and NOT:

```
extension Person {
    static var isMayorAndRecentlyModifiedPredicate: NSPredicate {
        return NSCompoundPredicate(andPredicateWithSubpredicates:
            [Person.isRecentlyModifiedPredicate, Person.isMayorPredicate])
    }
    static var isMayorOrRecentlyModifiedPredicate: NSPredicate {
        return NSCompoundPredicate(orPredicateWithSubpredicates:
            [Person.isRecentlyModifiedPredicate, Person.isMayorPredicate])
    }
}
```

To negate an existing predicate, we can use
NSCompoundPredicate(notPredicateWithSubpredicate:):

```
extension Person {
    static var notMayorPredicate: NSPredicate {
        return NSCompoundPredicate(
            notPredicateWithSubpredicate: Person.isMayorPredicate)
    }
}
```

Constant Predicates

The predicate format strings YES and NO, along with the corresponding TRUEPREDICATE and FALSEPREDICATE, let us build constant predicates. In code, we can also use the NSPredicate(value:_) initializer:

```
let predicate = NSPredicate(value: true)
```

These are useful as default values on predicate properties to conform to a specific protocol.

If the app allows some objects to be hidden, such entities might have a hidden attribute. We can abstract this for all entities — even those that don't have a hidden attribute — by defining a property called hiddenPredicate:

```
protocol Hideable {
    static var hiddenPredicate: NSPredicate { get }
}
```

```
extension Person: Hideable {
    static var hiddenPredicate: NSPredicate {
        return NSPredicate(format: "%K", Person.Keys.hidden.rawValue)
    }
}

extension City: Hideable {
    static var hiddenPredicate: NSPredicate {
        let  predicate = NSPredicate(value: true)
        return predicate
    }
}
```

Traversing Relationships

We can traverse relationships directly in predicates. Anywhere we use the %K specifier, we can use either a key or a so-called key path.

How we use these depends on whether the relationship is a to-one or a to-many relationship. Our *City* entity has a mayor relationship to Person. If we want to match cities based on the age of the mayor, we can use the mayor.age key path:

```
let  predicate = NSPredicate(format: "%K.%K > %lu",
    City.Keys.mayor.rawValue, Person.Keys.age.rawValue, 30)
```

When we're traversing a to-many relationship, there are (potentially) multiple objects at the other end of that relationship, e.g. a City object has multiple Person objects as its visitors. In such a case, we need to be more specific about how we want to match these objects.

One approach is to use an "any" match: a predicate to match a city where any visitor is younger than 21 needs to include the ANY keyword:

```
let  predicate = NSPredicate(format: "ANY %K.%K <= %lu",
    City.Keys.residents.rawValue, Person.Keys.age.rawValue, 20)
```

Subqueries

If we want to find cities where all residents are younger than 36, we have to rely on a subquery. Subqueries work a bit like a recursive fetch request, except that they're all executed within SQLite and hence relatively performant. They may be a bit unwieldy at first, but subqueries allow for very powerful query statements.

The most common way to use subqueries is to write a query for the target of the relationship, i.e. *Person*, and then check if the count is 0:

```
let predicate = NSPredicate(
    format: "(SUBQUERY(%K, $x, $x.%K >= %lu).@count == 0)",
    City.Keys.residents.rawValue, Person.Keys.age.rawValue, 36)
```

This results in the following:

```
SUBQUERY(residents, $x, $x.age >= 36).@count == 0
```

The first parameter, residents, is the name of the relationship for which we want to test elements. The second part, $x, is the variable we're using. Finally, the third part, $x.age >= 36, decides if the element will be included. $x inside this predicate is a *Person* object that's a resident in the *City*.

We then take the count of all matching residents and check if this count is 0. This, in effect, will give us all cities where all residents are younger than 36 — including cities without any residents.

Alternatively, we could have expressed this as the following:

```
SUBQUERY(residents, $x, $x.age < 36).@count == residents.@count
```

Another situation where we need to use subqueries is when we want to match on multiple attributes through a relationship. If we want to match all cities that have at least one resident who is both younger than 25 and owns 2 cars, we can do that with the following:

```
SUBQUERY(residents, $x, $x.age < 25 AND $x.carsOwnedCount == 2).@count != 0
```

```
ANY resident.age < 25 && ANY resident.carsOwnedCount == 2
```

This would match any city where there's a resident younger than 25 and there's a resident who owns 2 cars. But it will match regardless of whether these two are true for the same resident or distinct residents.

Matching Objects and Object IDs

A powerful feature of predicates is that we can match objects directly. We can do so by matching on either the object or its object identifier.

Directly matching an object may seem very odd. But if we execute a fetch request that matches the object, it will force Core Data to reload this object from the file system and update the row cache, and we can use this to make sure the object is not a fault:

```
let request = NSFetchRequest(entityName: Person.entityName)
request.predicate = NSPredicate(format: "self == %@", person)
request.returnsObjectsAsFaults = false
try! moc.executeFetchRequest(request)
```

Be sure to read the performance chapter to fully understand the implications of the above.

We can do the same for matching multiple objects of the same entity by using the IN operator and passing an array or a set of objects:

```
let predicate = NSPredicate(format: "self IN %@", somePeople)
```

In both cases, we could have passed in an object ID or a managed object. Either way, Core Data turns these predicates into SQL statements that will match the primary key for the passed-in object(s).

We can also use this while traversing relationships. If we have a *Person* object, we can use it to match *City* objects that this person has visited:

```
let predicate = NSPredicate(format: "%K CONTAINS %@",
    City.Keys.visitors.rawValue, person)
```

But this is quite pointless on its own, since we would have been better off by just traversing the relationship citiesVisited from the *Person* to *City*. It can be useful, though, if we need to combine it with other predicates:

```
let predicate = NSPredicate(format: "%K CONTAINS %@ AND %K.@count >= 3",
    City.Keys.visitors.rawValue, person, City.Keys.visitors.rawValue)
```

Matching Strings

When it comes to matching strings, things are more complicated. Core Data has powerful support for most kinds of string matching and comparison, but quite often this will not work in the way the user expects. This is because text in and of itself is complex — so complex that we have dedicated an entire chapter to it. Be sure that you have read the text chapter and that you understand what your app needs to support and what doesn't matter for your specific case.

There are generally two different cases: one is *user-visible* text, and the other one is text that's only to be interpreted by the computer. If you want to search for or compare user-visible text, the text chapter will tell you which approach is best.

For text that is not visible to the user, we will outline a few possibilities and things to be aware of. This will apply to text that is used as an internal identifier between your app and your backend, or keys that are text based. This kind of text is ASCII and hence a lot easier to reason about.

The key takeaway is to always use the [n] string option after the comparison operator in order to tell Core Data that the strings are ASCII. n is short for normalized.

The predicates playground[2] has a page about strings that shows how string matching can be used. It has a *Country* entity with an attribute called alpha3Code, which contains the country's ISO 3166-1 alpha-3 code.

We can match a specific country with ==[n]:

```
let predicate = NSPredicate(format: "%K ==[n] %@",
    Country.Keys.alpha3Code.rawValue, "ZAF")
```

This search is very efficient if we add an index on the given attribute. Its performance is comparable to searching for an integer attribute that has an index.

Similarly, the BEGINSWITH[n], ENDSWITH[n], and CONTAINS[n] operators search for strings with a specific prefix, suffix, or part:

```
let predicate = NSPredicate(format: "%K BEGINSWITH[n] %@",
    Country.Keys.alpha3Code.rawValue, "CA")

let predicate = NSPredicate(format: "%K ENDSWITH[n] %@",
    Country.Keys.alpha3Code.rawValue, "K")

let predicate = NSPredicate(format: "%K CONTAINS[n] %@",
    Country.Keys.alpha3Code.rawValue, "IN")
```

The LIKE[n] and MATCHES[n] operators allow for more complexity, but as a result, these are also more expensive to use on a database with many rows:

```
let predicate = NSPredicate(format: "%K LIKE[n] %@",
    Country.Keys.alpha3Code.rawValue, "?A?")

let predicate = NSPredicate(format: "%K MATCHES[n] %@",
    Country.Keys.alpha3Code.rawValue, "[AB][FLH](.)")
```

Finally, the IN[n] operator matches if a string attribute is contained in the given array of strings:

```
let predicate = NSPredicate(format: "%K IN[n] %@",
    Country.Keys.alpha3Code.rawValue, ["FRA", "FIN", "ISL"])
```

Strings and Indexes

The [n] option tells Core Data that the text strings can be compared byte for byte. This, in turn, allows SQLite to use an index for the given attribute, if one is available. The performance chapter and the profiling chapter go into more details about the tradeoffs of indexes and how to measure if adding one improves performance.

The predicate operators ==[n], BEGINSWITH[n], and IN[n] are all able to use an index on the given attribute. As a result, they'll perform well even on large datasets, as long as the attribute has an index.

On the other hand, ENDSWITH[n], CONTAINS[n], LIKE[n], and MATCHES[n] will not benefit from an index. They do, in fact, rely on SQLite calling into Core Data for each value, as SQLite scans the entire table. Consequently, these operators will likely be quite expensive on large datasets.

As a result, try to rely on the ==[n], BEGINSWITH[n], and IN[n] operators whenever possible.

Transformable Values

When using transformable attributes with Core Data, we can directly use predicates on their keys.

The *City* entity in the sample playground has a property called remoteIdentifier that is an optional NSUUID. It is implemented as a transformable attribute with a custom NSValueTransformer that transforms between an NSUUID and the corresponding binary data.

When we create a predicate to match a specific remoteIdentifier, we can pass in an NSUUID object. Core Data will do the transformation to binary data for us and create the corresponding query in SQLite:

```
let  identifier :  NSUUID = allRemoteIdentifiers.first!
let  predicate = NSPredicate(format: "%K == %@",
    City.Keys.remoteIdentifier.rawValue, identifier)
```

You can even compare transformable values with the inequality operators ⟨, ⟩, etc. Whether or not these comparisons make sense depends on the values being compared and on the way they're transformed into binary data. The result is equivalent to what memcmp(3) on the binary data would consider larger or smaller.

Performance and Ordering Expressions

We explained in the performance chapter why executing fetch requests is expensive: mainly because they (by API contract) always have to consult SQLite and the storage in the file system. Once you work with a large dataset, the way the predicate is constructed and the existence of indexes will also have an important impact on the performance of fetch requests that use predicates. Be sure to check out the profiling chapter — it goes into quite a bit of detail about how to inspect and debug the performance profile of fetch requests using the EXPLAIN QUERY PLAN command.

When constructing complex predicates, it's a good idea to put simple and/or performant parts first and more complex ones later. For example, if a predicate checks both the age and the carsOwnedCount attributes, and we know that we only have an index on age, it would generally be better to put this part first in the predicate:

```
let predicate = NSPredicate(format: "%K > %ld && %K == %ld",
    Person.Keys.age.rawValue, 32,
    Person.Keys.carsOwnedCount.rawValue, 2)
```

Along the same lines, it can be beneficial to put the part of a predicate that we know will limit the dataset the most first. If we want to find those *Person* objects where hidden is **true** and age > 30, we may know that due to the way our app works, only very few objects have hidden set to **true**, while age > 30 will match most objects. It would therefore be better to put the part that checks for hidden first, so that it limits the dataset as much as possible before we have to evaluate age > 30:

```
let predicate = NSPredicate(format: "%K == YES && %K > %ld",
    Person.Keys.hidden.rawValue,
    Person.Keys.age.rawValue, 30)
```

Quite often, though, the largest win may come from creating appropriate indexes. Indexes don't come for free. Be sure to read both the section about indexes in the performance chapter and the profiling chapter in general. If you want to improve performance, the only correct way is to measure before and after each change and compare the results — something that is described in these chapters.

Summary

Predicates provide a compact and easy way to describe what subset of objects we're interested in. They provide a lot of flexibility.

We showed how it's best not to hardcode attribute names, and how combining predicates into compound predicates ensures that we don't repeat predicate code. We also discussed the ability to traverse both to-one and to-many relationships, and how doing so allows for very powerful searches, particularly with subqueries. Finally, we touched upon string matching. For text that's visible to the user, we refer to the text chapter. For text that's not visible to the user (keys, codes, etc.), we showed a wide range of possibilities.

Text

11

Storing text in Core Data is straightforward. Searching and sorting text strings, on the other hand, can be quite complex. Due to the intricacies of both Unicode and languages, the concept of two text strings being equal is very different from that of their underlying bytes being equal. And figuring out which string comes before another one is rather complicated too; it heavily depends on the locale at hand.

Some Examples

Dealing with text is hard, and this chapter is not an extensive discussion of Unicode. For that, there are plenty of outside resources worth reading. We suggest objc.io's article on Unicode as a good starting point, while the homepage of The Unicode Consortium is a great resource for all the scary details. For the purpose of this chapter, however, we will just look at a few examples to illustrate the problems of the domain.

Let's assume that we have a *City* entity with a name property, and in our app, the user can search for a city by its name.

The 14th-largest city in France is *Saint-Étienne*. When a user types Saint-Étienne into the search field, we want to match this city with our search predicate. The problem is that the letter "É" can be represented in Unicode in two ways: either as the single code point U+00C9 (*E with acute accent*), or as the pair of code points U+0301 U+0045 (*Combining acute accent* followed by a regular *E*). From the user's perspective, these are identical. Additionally, the user would expect to find the city even if the name is entered in lowercase, e.g. saint-étienne. And maybe the search string Saint Etienne should match too. The point is, these are all very different byte strings. They will not be considered equal using a simple comparison, even though the user may expect them to be.

In some locales, a user would expect the Danish city *Aarhus* to be found when entering the search string *Århus*. The letter Å can either be represented by U+00C5 (*A with ring above*) or by U+030A U+0041 (*Combining ring above* followed by *A*). Meanwhile, in non-Latin scripts, we have to ask ourselves if the corresponding Latin text is supposed to match. Should the user be able to find the Chinese city of 西安 by entering "Xi'an?" And what about the ' (U+0027) in this name? Should it be matched if the user enters ' (U+2019) as a search string?

The answers to these questions are highly domain specific. Solving all of these problems can get very complicated, but it's essential to know which ones to solve and which ones not to solve for the given problem at hand. It may be important for your app that saint-etienne matches Saint-Étienne, but totally fine that Århus does not match Aarhus.

Similar problems arise for sorting. Even with just the Latin script, things are more difficult than first meets the eye. When looking at individual letters, it is obvious that *B* comes after *A*. But things can be different when looking at complete words. And the sort order depends on the user's locale — which language the user's operating system is set to use.

Just within Germany, there are two sort orders for the letter "ö": it is considered equal to either "o" or "oe." In German, *Köln* is sorted before *Kyllburg*. In Swedish, however, the letter "ö" follows all other letters so that *Sundsvall* would be sorted before *Södertälje*.

A Danish user would expect the cities *Viborg*, *Ølstykke-Stenløse*, and *Aarhus* to be in this order. This is because the letter "Ø" follows the letter "Z," and the double "A" is semantically equivalent to the letter "Å," which is the last letter in the Danish alphabet.

When mixing scripts, should "Москва" be ordered before or after all names in the Latin script? Or should it be intermixed, i.e. "Москва" next to "Madrid?"

Again, the answer depends on the domain, i.e. what problem the app is trying to solve.

It is also important to note that in programming, there are situations where we're using text strings that are not going to be visible to the user. If a text string is just an identifier or a key not visible in the UI, we may not want *art* to match *Art*.

Searching

If the number of entries that we have to search is very small, it is totally fine to take advantage of NSPredicate's ability to perform comparisons that ignore letter case and diacritics:

```
let predicate = NSPredicate(format: "%K BEGINSWITH[cd] %@",
    City.nameKey, searchTerm)
```

The BEGINSWITH operator matches any values that start with the search term. The [cd] modifiers specify that the search should be case insensitive and ignore diacritics such as accents or umlauts. This will ensure that the search term saint-etienne will match the Saint-Étienne entry.

However, when the database has many rows, this way of matching entries becomes very expensive. The case-insensitive and diacritic-insensitive search we requested with BEGINSWITH[cd] is a fairly complex Unicode operation that is implemented by NSString. Because SQLite cannot do this comparison natively, it has to read each database entry and pass it to Core Data to perform the comparison. If there are 12,812 entries in the database, all 12,812 names will be read off the file system to be passed to Core Data individually.

And because the comparison has to be done in a function, SQLite cannot use any index to speed it up. The performance chapter explains why searches in large databases benefit from adding an index for the attribute in question. But when we're using BEGINSWITH[cd], this is not possible.

String Normalization

In order to be able to do efficient searches in larger datasets, we need to normalize the string attributes we want to perform searches on. We will change our data model so that the *City* entity will have both a name and a name_normalized attribute. In the code for the City class, we will only expose the name property. But we will add logic so that the name_normalized attribute gets updated whenever the name changes:

```
final public class City : NSManagedObject {
    public static let nameKey = "name"
    public static let normalizedNameKey = "name_normalized"
    @NSManaged private var primitiveName: String
    public var name: String {
        set {
            willChangeValueForKey(City.nameKey)
            primitiveName = newValue
            updateNormalizedName(newValue)
            didChangeValueForKey(City.nameKey)
        }
        get {
            willAccessValueForKey(City.nameKey)
            let value = primitiveName
            didAccessValueForKey(City.nameKey)
            return value
```

```
        }
    }
    private func updateNormalizedName(name: String) {
        setValue(name.normalizedForSearch, forKey: City.normalizedNameKey)
    }
}

extension String {
    public var normalizedForSearch: String {
        return self  // Normalization logic goes here
    }
}
```

The normalizedForSearch extension will do the normalization (we'll look at
that in a bit). Inside the City class, we've added a primitiveName property,
which is **private**, i.e. only visible to this file. The name property is now
implemented *by hand* using that property. Note how primitiveName is
@NSManaged — it is implemented dynamically by Core Data. But the name
property is no longer **@NSManaged** — it is implemented in code. The new
code for the name property basically does the same as Core Data would have
otherwise done for us, with the one addition of calling
updateNormalizedName(_:). This function will set the normalized name.
Finally, we expose the key for the normalized name so that other code can
build an NSPredicate based on it.

This is quite a bit of code, but note how almost all of it is **private** to this file. To
the outside, there's just the *normal* name and the new
City.normalizedNameKey to be used for searching.

To normalize the string, take a look at the API for Unicode transformations
that is built into the Foundation framework. In this example, we make the
string lowercase, strip all diacritics, and convert non-Latin scripts to Latin as
defined by the Unicode standard's transforms, all in a single method call:

```
extension String {
    public var normalizedForSearch: String {
        let transformed = stringByApplyingTransform(
            "Any-Latin; Latin-ASCII; Lower", reverse: false)
        return transformed as String? ?? ""
    }
}
```

With this, "saint-étienne" and "Saint-Etienne" will both find "Saint-Étienne." And because we normalize both the values in the database and the search string, the Cyrillic "Москва" will still find "Москва."

The stringByApplyingTransform method on NSString is new in iOS 9 and OS X 10.11, but the functionality has been there for years. If you need to target older versions, you can use the equivalent CFStringTransform API in Core Foundation. The standard Unicode transforms are very powerful and, in most situations, probably better than what you can write yourself. But whether or not this approach works for your particular app is, of course, domain specific. To learn more about what you can do with Unicode transforms, check out the ICU User Guide.

In some cases, it may also be desirable to remove any non-letter characters from the normalized string. That can be done by using this transform instead:

```
Any-Latin; Latin-ASCII; Lower; [:^Letter:] Remove
```

With this code, "saint etienne" would find "Saint-Étienne" because they'd both be normalized to "saintetienne."

Efficient Searching

Since we now have normalized strings in the database, we can use a very efficient form of the predicate:

```
let predicate = NSPredicate(format: "%K BEGINSWITH[n] %@",
    City.normalizedNameKey, searchTerm.normalizedForSearch)
```

By adding the modifier [n] to the BEGINSWITH operator, we tell Core Data that the predicate's arguments have been normalized and therefore can be compared byte for byte, directly inside SQLite. There is no need to fetch all rows and perform an expensive Unicode-aware comparison. Note that we're passing in the key for the normalized name, and we're also normalizing the search term before passing it to the predicate.

For example, if the user searches for "Béziers," the final predicate will look like this:

```
name_normalized BEGINSWITH[n] "beziers"
```

Because the comparison can now be made directly by SQLite, we can speed it up even more by adding an index for the name_normalized attribute. This was not possible with the non-normalized approach.

With all this, searching in a list of about 4,000 cities is 10 to 15 times faster than the primitive version. With larger datasets, the speedup will be even more noticeable.

Sorting

In some situations, we need to sort objects by a text attribute. We might, for example, want to display a list of contacts sorted by their names. In these cases, we need to use a Unicode-aware and locale-specific collation.

The Foundation framework can sort strings according to the Unicode collation rules while respecting the current locale that the app is running in. But it is an expensive operation and has to be performed in memory; SQLite cannot help us with this. The Unicode Technical Standard #10 outlines some of the complexities of sorting text.

With this in mind, it is important to know how big the dataset is and how likely changes are. Both of these impact what the correct approach is: for small datasets, and when changes are rare, we can choose relatively simple solutions. But when the dataset is big, or we're expecting changes to happen frequently, we may need to take extra steps to make sure performance is good. We will now look at a few approaches and solutions. Which one is the proper fit depends a lot on the needs and domain of the app.

A Naive Approach

When requesting items from Core Data through a fetch request, we should always use an NSSortDescriptor on the fetch request to let SQLite do the sorting for us. Sadly, there's no easy and efficient method to sort strings in the way the user would expect.

The naive approach would be to write something like this:

```
let sd = NSSortDescriptor(key: City.nameKey, ascending: true)
request.sortDescriptors = [sd]
```

This would sort the entries by the byte values of their encodings — probably UTF-8. But for an app catered toward international users, this would not do the right thing.

If we only ever have to deal with a very small number of objects, we can do the sorting in memory. For instance, if our app is only ever going to have 100 cities, we might want to keep all of them in memory all of the time anyway. (We already mentioned this strategy in the section on small datasets in the performance chapter.) And if all objects are in memory anyway, we can simply sort them with the following:

```
cities.sortInPlace { (cityA, cityB) -> Bool in
    cityA.name.localizedStandardCompare(cityB.name) == .OrderedAscending
}
```

This sorting is very expensive. The string comparison has to take a lot of locale-specific conventions into account. On a 2.7 GHz Intel Core i7 MacBook Pro, sorting approximately 4,000 cities takes about 300 ms, or one-third of a second.

That time may be longer than we can afford if we re-sort every time our app accesses the collection of cities. A natural next step would be to keep the sorted array in memory at all times. This removes the performance bottleneck, but now we are responsible for keeping this array in sync with the persistent store. We'll look into ways to keep the sorted array around across app launches in a bit.

Updating a Sorted Array

If the array of cities changes — or if we change the name of a city — we need to re-sort the array. First, we need to detect if any City objects were inserted or changed. We can do this by listening to the NSManagedObjectContextObjectsDidChangeNotification. We need to check if the context for this notification is relevant to us — other frameworks might also use Core Data. Then we can look at the managed context's inserted and changed objects. If any City objects were inserted, we need to re-sort. If any City objects have their name properties changed, we also need to re-sort.

If we look at the inserted objects (NSInsertedObjectsKey) in the notification, we can filter these by their entities to see if any of them are *City* entities. We need to do the same for refreshed objects (NSRefreshedObjectsKey) — these could potentially represent objects that have been changed in another context.

Once the resulting save notification gets merged into our context, such objects will be refreshed. Finally, we need to check if any updated objects are cities and had their name properties changed:

```
guard let moc = note.object as? NSManagedObjectContext
else { fatalError("No context?") }

let hasInsertedOrRefreshedCities = { () -> Bool in
    let refreshed = note.userInfo?[NSRefreshedObjectsKey]
        as? Set<NSManagedObject>
    let inserted = note.userInfo?[NSInsertedObjectsKey]
        as? Set<NSManagedObject>
    func setContainsCity(set: Set<NSManagedObject>?) -> Bool {
        if let set = set {
            guard let cityEntity = moc.persistentStoreCoordinator?
                .managedObjectModel.entitiesByName["City"]
                else { fatalError("Must have entity") }
            for mo in set {
                if mo.entity === cityEntity {
                    return true
                }
            }
        }
        return false
    }
    return setContainsCity(refreshed) || setContainsCity(inserted)
}()

let hasCitiesWithUpdatedName = { () -> Bool in
    guard let updated = note.userInfo?[NSUpdatedObjectsKey]
        as? Set<NSManagedObject>
        else { return false }
    guard let cityEntity = moc.persistentStoreCoordinator?
        .managedObjectModel.entitiesByName["City"]
        else { fatalError("Must have entity") }
    for mo in updated {
        if mo.entity === cityEntity {
            if let _ = mo.changedValuesForCurrentEvent()[City.nameKey] {
                return true
            }
        }
    }
    return false
}()
```

```
// Invalidate the cache of sorted cities for context 'moc' here.
```

This is a lot of code, but it allows us to maintain an in-memory cache of sorted City objects and keep it up to date when changes occur.

We can take advantage of built-in NSArray features to make updating the cache after inserts and updates even faster. With a sorted array, we can use binary search to find the correct index point for inserting a new object. This is a very fast operation compared to re-sorting the array. The indexOfObject(_:inSortedRange:options:usingComparator:) method on NSArray implements the binary search algorithm.

Likewise, re-sorting the array after one or more objects have been changed can be sped up by keeping track of a hint object that "remembers" the work that was already done in previous sorts:

```
class CitiesSortedByName {
    var hint: NSData?
    var sortedCities: NSArray?

    let comparator: NSComparator = { cityA, cityB in
        guard let cityA = cityA as? City
            else { fatalError("Object is not a 'City'") }
        guard let cityB = cityB as? City
            else { fatalError("Object is not a 'City'") }
        return cityA.name.localizedStandardCompare(cityB.name)
    }

    typealias CComparator =
        @convention(c) (AnyObject, AnyObject, UnsafeMutablePointer<Void>) -> Int
    let cComparator: CComparator = { (cityA, cityB, _) in
        guard let cityA = cityA as? City
            else { fatalError("Object is not a 'City'") }
        guard let cityB = cityB as? City
            else { fatalError("Object is not a 'City'") }
        let r = cityA.name.localizedStandardCompare(cityB.name)
        return r.rawValue
    }

    func didInsertCities(inserted: Set<City>) {
        guard let sorted = sortedCities else { return }
        let mutableSorted = NSMutableArray(array: sorted)
        for city in inserted {
            let range = NSMakeRange(0, mutableSorted.count)
```

```
            let index = mutableSorted.indexOfObject(city, inSortedRange: range,
                options: .InsertionIndex, usingComparator: comparator)
            mutableSorted.insertObject(city, atIndex: index)
        }
        sortedCities = mutableSorted
    }

    func didChangeCityNames() {
        guard let oldArray = sortedCities else { return }
        if let hint = hint {
            sortedCities = oldArray.sortedArrayUsingFunction(cComparator,
                context: nil, hint: hint)
        } else {
            sortedCities = oldArray.sortedArrayUsingFunction(cComparator,
                context: nil)
        }
        hint = sortedCities!.sortedArrayHint
    }
}
```

Persisting a Sorted Array

Because localized string sorting is relatively expensive, it may be desirable to
persist the ordered array. However, it is worth pointing out beforehand that
this ordering is not guaranteed to be identical between different versions of
the Foundation framework. And if the user switches the locale, the array
would have to be re-sorted as well.

If the app persists an array for localized string sorting across app launches, it
must check on every relaunch if the current value of
NSFoundationVersionNumber matches the one that was being used when the
array was last sorted. It must also check if NSLocale.currentLocale() still has
the same value for NSLocaleCollatorIdentifier:

```
extension NSLocale {
    static var currentCollatorIdentifier: String? {
        return currentLocale().objectForKey(NSLocaleCollatorIdentifier)
            as? String
    }
}
```

The easiest option to persist a sorted list is to create an owner entity that has
an ordered to-many relationship to the entity we want to sort. In our case, we

would create a *SortedCityOwner* entity that has an ordered to-many relationship to City. With this, inserting and updating cities becomes more expensive because we have to keep the relationship from this owner entity to the cities up to date. But retrieving a sorted list of cities after launch is a lot faster. It's a classical tradeoff between the cost of retrieving data and the cost of updating/changing data.

If we use an ordered to-many relationship, the above logic for tracking changes can ignore refreshed objects. If a context merges changes into another context, it would also merge the newly sorted relationship.

The SortedCityOwner would be a pseudo singleton (per context). The performance chapter has a section called singleton-like objects that describes how to use such a pseudo singleton efficiently. The logic shown above in CitiesSortedByName would then have to update the order of the objects in this singleton-like object.

Summary

In this chapter, we have looked at comparing and sorting text strings. Generic solutions to these problems can be very complicated, but the specific needs of our application often allow us to use a good middle ground between complexity and features.

Additionally, we have shown how adding a normalized version of text attributes can be done relatively simply, and how it improves search experiences for non-ASCII text.

Sorting, on the other hand, is a non-trivial problem. We showed how small datasets can get away with a simple approach. We also demonstrated how apps with larger datasets and frequent changes can cache sort results in memory or in the file system to reduce the impact of expensive sorting.

Takeaways

→ Always use normalized strings for text that is searchable by the user.

→ Only add indexes to normalized string attributes.

→ Use the [n] modifier when comparing normalized strings.

→ Sorting user-facing text is very expensive.

Model Versions and Migrating Data

12

We already mentioned in the relationships chapter that opening an SQLite store file with a data model that doesn't match the contents of the database will cause an exception. This is where versioned data models and migrations come in. As an app grows and new features are added over time, the data model must adapt to the new requirements, e.g. by adding new attributes. Rather than simply changing the data model in place, we create new versions of the model and migrate existing data from the old model to the new model. In this chapter, we will go into details about how this works.

This chapter refers to a separate example project on GitHub[1] where we take the *Moody* data model through a series of migrations, showcasing the different techniques available. The project contains a test target[2], which tests the migration of pre-populated SQLite stores by comparing the results to hardcoded test fixtures. We'll talk more about the test setup later on.

Before we dive into the topic of migrations itself, we'd like to encourage you to consider whether or not you really need to migrate existing data. Migrations add an extra layer of complexity and maintenance work to your application. For example, if you're using Core Data only as an offline cache for data from a web service, you might get away with deleting the local data, creating a fresh store, and pulling the data you need from the backend again. Obviously there are many cases where you *do* need to migrate, but it's still worth thinking about this before you get started.

Model Versions

Up until now, we've only worked with a single version of the data model. Although we made frequent changes to the model during the development of our app, we never bothered with model versioning, since it's much easier during the initial development phase to simply delete old store files and start with a fresh store. Once we decide to make a change to the data model while the app is already used in production, we no longer have that luxury. Instead, we have to create a new model version.

To create a new version of your data model, open the .xcdatamodel file in Xcode and select Editor > Add Model ...Version. You'll be prompted to enter a name of the new version and to select the data model to base this version on.

---

1 https://github.com/objcio/core-data/blob/master/Migrations
2 https://github.com/objcio/core-data/blob/master/Migrations/MigrationTests

Once you have multiple versions in your data model file, you can select the
current version in Xcode's file inspector:

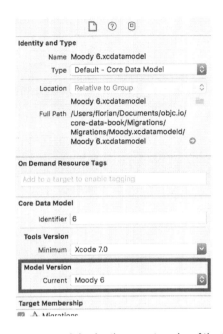

Figure 12.1: Selecting the current version of the data model in the file inspector

Core Data's data model file (.xcdatamodeld) is actually a package, which in
and of itself can contain several .xcdatamodel packages representing different
versions of the data model. When you compile your app, the data model will
be compiled into a .momd package, which contains one .mom file per model
version, as well as an optimized file variant (.omo) of the current model
version. We can load any previous data model we need during the migration
process from this versioned model file:

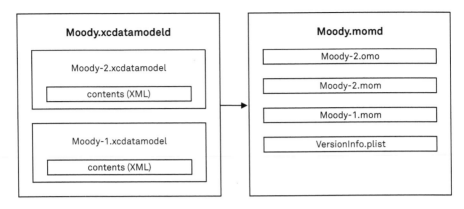

Figure 12.2: The source and compiled formats of a managed object model

In addition to the .mom and .omo files, the .momd package also contains a
VersionInfo.plist file. This plist specifies the current model version and
contains the hash values of all entities in all model versions. Those hash
values are calculated from all the properties that affect how an entity is stored
in SQLite. When you first create an SQLite store, Core Data stores those hash
values in the SQLite file. On every subsequent load of the store, it uses those
hash values to determine whether or not an existing store file can be opened
with a specific managed object model version.

You can give each model version a unique name and assign an identifier in the
file inspector, but at the end of the day, this information is really just for your
own purposes. Core Data relies on the version hashes to determine
compatibility between a store file and a managed object model.

One consequence of this is that we sometimes have to give Core Data a little
extra hint to pick up a new model version. If the change in the model doesn't
affect the structure of the SQLite database, it will be not reflected in the
entities' version hashes, and Core Data may assume compatibility between a
store and a model that actually aren't compatible.

For example, when we change the class name for an entity or the internal
format of a binary attribute, we have to specify a unique *hash modifier* for the
attribute or the entity in question. Core Data will include this modifier in the
calculation of the version hashes. This allows us to create a new model version,
which, although we haven't made any structural changes, is incompatible with
old versions:

Figure 12.3: Specifying hash modifiers forces Core Data to consider the data model as changed, even if its structure hasn't

When you make structural changes to your data model, you can just leave this field empty.

The Migration Process

Once you've defined a new model version, you need to think about how to migrate data from the old model to the new one. That's what a *migration* does in Core Data terms: it moves the data from an SQLite database created with one model to a new SQLite database created with a different model.

How an old model maps to a new model is defined by a *mapping model* that is specific to those two model versions. It describes which entities or attributes should be copied, renamed, transformed, etc.

There are two fundamentally different ways to create a mapping model. If the changes from one model to the other can be expressed in terms of a limited set of simple transformations, you can let Core Data infer the mapping model for you. This is called a *lightweight migration*. If the changes you want to make are more complex, you have to create a custom mapping model.

We'll go into more detail for both types of mapping models below, but first we'll discuss some general considerations with regard to the migration process.

When you call addPersistentStoreWithType(_:configuration:URL:options:) on a coordinator and pass **nil** for the options dictionary, an exception will be thrown if the specified store doesn't match the coordinator's model version. This is the point at which the migration process needs to kick in to get the SQLite store into the format that's understood by the coordinator.

At this point you have two options: either let Core Data take care of the migration process, or manually control the migration. The former option is much simpler but has some limitations, which we'll explain shortly.

Automatic Migration

To tell Core Data to take charge of the migration, set NSMigratePersistentStoresAutomaticallyOption to **true** in the options dictionary when adding the persistent store. If the store file doesn't match the coordinator's model version, Core Data will then try to locate an appropriate mapping model within the application bundles and start the migration. Once the migration is done, it will open the persistent store as usual.

If you also set NSInferMappingModelAutomaticallyOption to **true**, Core Data will try to infer a mapping model in case it can't locate one. This will succeed if the changes between the two models can be bridged by a lightweight migration. We'll describe the exact requirements for this below.

Using these two options makes the migration process extremely simple. However, as mentioned above, this approach also comes with some limitations.

Automatic migration is always performed in one single step from the old to the new model version. This means that you have to provide mapping models for all potential combinations: when you add your second version, you only have to provide one mapping model. But when you add a third version, you already have to provide two new mapping models (from the first and the second version to the current one). The next time, it's already up to three new mapping models. This obviously does not scale well. Whether or not that is a problem for you depends on how often your model changes and how complex those changes are.

Additionally, the one-step migration process prevents you from migrating subsets of data independently, which can be useful if your dataset is extremely large.

Manual Migration

For more flexibility, we can control the migration process ourselves. This allows us to perform progressive migrations, i.e. migrating an existing store by iteratively transforming it from its current version to its successor model version. This solution scales much better with frequent model changes.

In the migrations test project[3], we use the manual approach. It allows us to explain each part of the migration process, thereby providing a much deeper understanding of how it works.

Before we get to the custom migration code itself, we'll first take a step back and revisit the topic of model versions. Above, we've only shown how to create new model versions in Xcode's data model editor. Now we want to make those model versions and how they relate to each other explicit in code. This will make model versioning clearer and the actual migration code simpler.

Handling Model Versions Explicitly

Model versions are identified by the names you've given them. We'll have to access the different model versions from our migration code. To make this easier, we define an enum that lists all model versions with the underlying string value representing each version's name:

```
enum ModelVersion: String {
    case Version1 = "Moody"
    case Version2 = "Moody 2"
}
```

Now we add some helper functionality to this enum with the ModelVersionType protocol:

```
public protocol ModelVersionType: Equatable {
    static var AllVersions: [Self] { get }
    static var CurrentVersion: Self { get }
    var name: String { get }
    var successor: Self? { get }
    var modelBundle: NSBundle { get }
    var modelDirectoryName: String { get }
    func mappingModelsToSuccessor() -> [NSMappingModel]?
```

---

3 https://github.com/objcio/core-data/blob/master/Migrations

```
}
```

To make the ModelVersion enum conform to this protocol, we just need to add
a couple of properties:

```
extension ModelVersion: ModelVersionType {
    static var AllVersions: [ModelVersion] { return [.Version2, .Version1] }
    static var CurrentVersion: ModelVersion { return .Version2 }

    var name: String { return rawValue }
    var modelBundle: NSBundle { return NSBundle(forClass: Mood.self) }
    var modelDirectoryName: String { return "Moody.momd" }

    var successor: ModelVersion? {
        switch self {
        case .Version1: return .Version2
        default: return nil
        }
    }
}
```

Now the ModelVersion enum encapsulates all the information related to the
data model: the names of the models, where they reside, and how they relate
to each other. This makes it easy to define useful extensions on
ModelVersionType in order to, for example, load a specific version of the
model:

```
extension ModelVersionType {
    public func managedObjectModel() -> NSManagedObjectModel {
        let omoURL = modelBundle.URLForResource(name,
            withExtension: "omo", subdirectory: modelDirectoryName)
        let momURL = modelBundle.URLForResource(name,
            withExtension: "mom", subdirectory: modelDirectoryName)
        guard let url = omoURL ?? momURL else {
            fatalError("model version \(self) not found")
        }
        guard let model = NSManagedObjectModel(contentsOfURL: url) else {
            fatalError("cannot open model at \(url)")
        }
        return model
    }
}
```

We can also add a handy initializer to get the version of an existing store file:

```
extension ModelVersionType {
    public init ?(storeURL: NSURL) {
        guard let metadata = try? NSPersistentStoreCoordinator
            .metadataForPersistentStoreOfType(NSSQLiteStoreType,
                URL: storeURL, options: nil) else
        {
            return nil
        }
        let version = Self.AllVersions.findFirstOccurence {
            $0.managedObjectModel().isConfiguration(nil,
                compatibleWithStoreMetadata: metadata)
        }
        guard let result  = version else { return nil }
        self = result
    }
}
```

We'll add even more functionality to this protocol as we go forward. (You can find the full source code of the migrations test project on GitHub[4].)

With this explicit definition of model versions in place, the code to perform manual progressive migrations becomes pretty straightforward to write.

Progressive Migrations

Our goal is to build a simple function that takes a source URL, a destination URL, and a target model version as arguments and performs the necessary migration steps:

```
public func migrateStoreFromURL<Version: ModelVersionType>(
    sourceURL: NSURL, toURL: NSURL, targetVersion: Version,
    deleteSource: Bool = false, progress: NSProgress? = nil)
{
    // ...
}
```

The first step is to figure out the mapping models we need to apply in order to get from the store's current version to the target version. For this, we define an extension on ModelVersionType to retrieve the mapping models that get us from one version to its immediate successor:

4 https://github.com/objcio/core-data/blob/master/Migrations

```
extension ModelVersionType {
    public func mappingModelsToSuccessor() -> [NSMappingModel]? {
        guard let nextVersion = successor else { return nil }
        guard let mapping = NSMappingModel(fromBundles: [modelBundle],
            forSourceModel: managedObjectModel(),
            destinationModel: nextVersion.managedObjectModel())
            else { fatalError("no mapping from \(self) to \(nextVersion)") }
        return [mapping]
    }
}
```

This method returns an array of mapping models, because we could split up a single migration step into multiple mapping models, as outlined in Apple's documentation. This can reduce memory pressure when migrating very large datasets.

With the mappingModelsToSuccessor() helper method, it's easy to define another extension that returns all the migration steps for a certain target model version:

```
public struct MigrationStep {
    var sourceModel: NSManagedObjectModel
    var destinationModel: NSManagedObjectModel
    var mappingModels: [NSMappingModel]
}
```

```
extension ModelVersionType {
    public func migrationStepsToVersion(version: Self) -> [MigrationStep] {
        guard self != version else { return [] }
        guard let mappings = mappingModelsToSuccessor(),
            let nextVersion = successor else
        {
            fatalError("couldn't find  mapping models")
        }
        let step = MigrationStep(sourceModel: managedObjectModel(),
            destinationModel: nextVersion.managedObjectModel(),
            mappingModels: mappings)
        return [step] + nextVersion.migrationStepsToVersion(version)
    }
}
```

This method returns an empty array if we're already at the target version. If we're not there yet, we make sure that a mapping model to the next version exists (otherwise we have made a mistake) and call migrationStepsToVersion(_:) recursively. This way, we end up with an array of MigrationStep objects, each one encapsulating the source model, the destination model, and the mapping models for this particular step in the process.

Now we can write the migrateStoreFromURL(_:toURL:targetVersion:) function like this:

```
public func migrateStoreFromURL<Version: ModelVersionType>(
    sourceURL: NSURL, toURL: NSURL, targetVersion: Version,
    deleteSource: Bool = false, progress: NSProgress? = nil)
{
    guard let sourceVersion = Version(storeURL: sourceURL) else {
        fatalError("unknown store version at URL \(sourceURL)")
    }
    var currentURL = sourceURL
    let migrationSteps = sourceVersion.migrationStepsToVersion(targetVersion)
    for step in migrationSteps {
        let manager = NSMigrationManager(sourceModel: step.sourceModel,
            destinationModel: step.destinationModel)
        let destinationURL = NSURL.temporaryURL()
        for mapping in step.mappingModels {
            try! manager.migrateStoreFromURL(currentURL,
                type: NSSQLiteStoreType, options: nil,
                withMappingModel: mapping, toDestinationURL: destinationURL,
                destinationType: NSSQLiteStoreType, destinationOptions: nil)
        }
        if currentURL != sourceURL {
            NSPersistentStoreCoordinator.destroyStoreAtURL(currentURL)
        }
        currentURL = destinationURL
    }
    try! NSPersistentStoreCoordinator.replaceStoreAtURL(toURL,
        withStoreAtURL: currentURL)
    if (currentURL != sourceURL) {
        NSPersistentStoreCoordinator.destroyStoreAtURL(currentURL)
    }
    if (toURL != sourceURL && deleteSource) {
        NSPersistentStoreCoordinator.destroyStoreAtURL(sourceURL)
    }
}
```

In this function, we iterate over the MigrationStep array and use the NSMigrationManager to execute each step. We always use a temporary URL as destination URL for the migration and clean up behind ourselves after each successful step. Once all migration steps have been successfully executed, we copy the new store to its final destination URL. It's a good safety measure to only remove or overwrite the original store after the migration is done. In case we ever ship an app update where migration fails for some users, the original store file is still around, and we have a second chance to get things right with the next update.

We use **try**! on purpose for the calls that can throw errors. If a call to migrateStoreFromURL or replaceStoreAtURL fails, we've made a programming mistake and we want to crash immediately.

With this migration function in place, all that's left to do is to use it when opening the persistent store. For example, we can encapsulate this code in a convenience initializer of NSManagedObjectContext:

```
extension NSManagedObjectContext {
    public convenience init<Version: ModelVersionType>(
        concurrencyType: NSManagedObjectContextConcurrencyType,
        modelVersion: Version, storeURL: NSURL, progress: NSProgress? = nil)
    {
        if let storeVersion = Version(storeURL: storeURL)
            where storeVersion != modelVersion
        {
            migrateStoreFromURL(storeURL, toURL: storeURL,
                targetVersion: modelVersion, deleteSource: true,
                progress: progress)
        }
        let psc = NSPersistentStoreCoordinator(
            managedObjectModel: modelVersion.managedObjectModel())
        try! psc.addPersistentStoreWithType(NSSQLiteStoreType,
            configuration: nil, URL: storeURL, options: nil)
        self.init(concurrencyType: concurrencyType)
        persistentStoreCoordinator = psc
    }
}
```

You should always perform migrations on a background queue and provide progress reporting to the user (though we omitted both in the code above for the sake of simplicity). We'll come back to this in the section about migrations and the user interface.

Compared to the automatic migrations described above, manual migrations require quite a bit of additional work and code to maintain. Which path you should choose depends on your use case: if you only change the model infrequently during the lifetime of the application, the simpler automatic approach might be a better fit for your app.

Inferred Mapping Models

Core Data can infer the mapping model between two given model versions if the changes between them are limited to a set of simple transformations. Migrations using an inferred mapping model are also called *lightweight migrations*.

The following are transformations that can be handled by lightweight migrations:

→ Adding, removing, and renaming attributes

→ Adding, removing, and renaming relationships

→ Adding, removing, and renaming entities

→ Changing the optional status of attributes

→ Adding or removing indexes on attributes

→ Adding, removing, or changing compound indexes on entities

→ Adding, removing, or changing unique constraints on entities

There are a few gotchas to this list. First, if you change an attribute from optional to non-optional, you *have* to specify a default value. The second, more subtle pitfall is that changing indexes (on attributes as well as compound indexes) will not be picked up as a model change. You have to specify a hash modifier on the changed attributes or entities in order to force Core Data to do the right thing during migration.

When you rename attributes or entities, you have to use the renaming ID (in the data model inspector) to provide Core Data with a hint of the previous name. For example, in the first test migration in the migrations sample project[5], we rename the attribute remoteIdentifier in the first model version to remoteID in the second version. In order to make this work, we specify remoteIdentifier as the *renaming identifier* on the remoteID attribute in the second version. If we were to rename the property again in the third version,

---

5 https://github.com/objcio/core-data/blob/master/Migrations/MigrationsTests/MigrationTests.swift

we would have to specify the renaming identifier of the second version as renaming identifier of the third version, and so on.

If you're using the automatic migration process, you don't have to do anything more. Core Data will detect the existing model version and create an inferred mapping model to the new model. If you use a manual migration process, you can still use lightweight migrations, but you'll have to instantiate the inferred mapping model yourself. NSMappingModel provides the static inferredMappingModelForSourceModel(_:destinationModel:) method for this purpose.

In the migrations sample project[6], we use this method to create an inferred mapping model from the first to the second version of the data model:

```
extension ModelVersion: ModelVersionType {
    func mappingModelsToSuccessor() -> [NSMappingModel]? {
        switch self {
        case .Version1:
            let mapping =
                try! NSMappingModel.inferredMappingModelForSourceModel(
                    managedObjectModel(),
                    destinationModel: successor!.managedObjectModel())
            return [mapping]
            // ...
        }
    }
}
```

The call to create the inferred mapping model can throw an error. We use **try**! in order to crash immediately if that happens. If the mapping model cannot be inferred, then it's a programming error.

Custom Mapping Models

If you have to make deeper changes to your data model than what's possible with lightweight migrations, you have to create a mapping model that specifies the details of how the old data model maps to the new one. For example, you can combine separate entities into one, split existing entities, create new relationships between existing data, and much more.

---

6 https://github.com/objcio/core-data/blob/master/Migrations

While you can create mapping models in code, the usual approach is to use Xcode's mapping model editor. Choosing "Mapping Model" when creating a new file will prompt you for the source and destination models and pre-populate the new mapping model with the mappings for all the things that haven't changed:

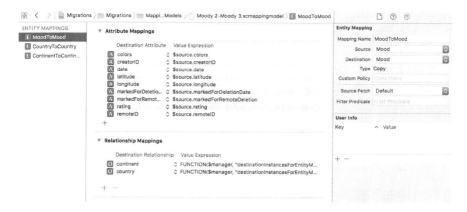

Figure 12.4: Xcode's mapping model editor

On the left-hand side, you have a list of all *entity mappings*. An entity mapping specifies how an entity in the source model maps to an entity in the destination model. If we add a new entity, the source entity is empty. If we remove an existing entity, the mapping for this source entity is either omitted completely or its destination entity is empty.

In the middle, you see a list of all the *property mappings*. These describe how each attribute and each relationship in the destination model map to the old model.

Finally, on the right-hand side, you can adjust the details of the selected mapping as usual.

As an example, let's take a look at the mapping model "Moody 4-Moody 5.xcmappingmodel"[7] in the sample project. In this migration, we remove the *Continent* entity altogether and add an isoContinent attribute on *Country* instead. isoContinent should contain the numeric identifier of the continent object formerly associated with the country.

---

7 https://github.com/objcio/core-data/blob/master/Migrations/Moody%204-Moody%205.xcmappingmodel

The value of each property mapping is an instance of NSExpression. For our purposes, we simply specify the following for the new isoContinent attribute:

```
$source.continent.numericISO3166Code
```

This instructs Core Data to get the value of the numericISO3166Code attribute of the currently migrated country's continent and use it as value for the new attribute.

For a more complex example, let's examine the mapping model shown in the screenshot above (this is the "Moody 2-Moody 3.xcmappingmodel"[8] file in the sample project). This mapping model describes how a new one-to-many relationship should be created between the *Continent* and the *Mood* entities. The *MoodToMood* entity mapping contains a property mapping describing the new continent relationship with the following expression:

```
FUNCTION($manager,
    "destinationInstancesForEntityMappingNamed:sourceInstances:",
    "ContinentToContinent", $source.country.continent)
```

This expression calls the destinationInstancesForEntityMappingNamed(_:sourceInstances:) method on the migration manager to get the managed object in the destination store that corresponds to the mood's continent object in the source store. The $manager variable refers to the migration manager. The $source variable refers to the source object that's currently being migrated, so we can use that to get to the source mood's continent by specifying $source.country.continent.

The inverse of this new relationship is the moods relationship on the *Continent* entity. We specify the value expression for the moods relationship in the *ContinentToContinent* entity mapping as the following:

```
FUNCTION($manager,
    "destinationInstancesForEntityMappingNamed:sourceInstances:",
    "MoodToMood", $source.countries.@distinctUnionOfSets.moods)
```

This is very similar to the continent relationship above, but it makes use of the @distinctUnionOfSets collection operator available through key-value coding. The operator works similarly to the flatMap method for collections in Swift: it flattens the nested set of sets of moods per country into a single set that

8 https://github.com/objcio/core-data/blob/master/Migrations/Moody%202-Moody%203.xcmappingmodel

contains all moods of all countries of the continent being migrated. It's a convenient way to remove the extra level of indirection the countries relationship provided between continents and moods.

If you can't achieve what you need by specifying expressions for the new attributes and relationships in the mapping model editor, you can go one step further and specify a custom NSEntityMigrationPolicy subclass for each entity mapping to get full control over the process. We'll look at an example of this next.

Custom Entity Mapping Policies

With custom entity mapping policies, you gain full control over the migration process. In the migrations sample project, we create an NSEntityMigrationPolicy subclass called Country5ToCountry6Policy[9] to split the *Country* entity with its numeric isoContinent attribute into a *Country* entity and a *Continent* entity, thereby establishing a new relationship between the two.

To tell Core Data to use our custom mapping policy, we have to specify its class name in the details inspector of the *CountryToCountry* entity mapping:

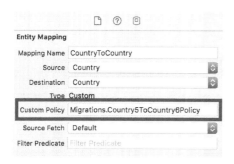

Figure 12.5: Specifying the name of a custom NSEntityMigrationPolicy subclass

NSEntityMigrationPolicy provides several methods you can override to customize the migration process. Please check Apple's documentation for all the details. In our example, we'll just override one of them, createDestinationInstancesForSourceInstance(_:entityMapping:manager:):

9 https://github.com/objcio/core-data/blob/master/Migrations/Migrations/Country5ToCountry6Policy.swift

```
class Country5ToCountry6Policy: NSEntityMigrationPolicy {
    override func createDestinationInstancesForSourceInstance(
        sInstance: NSManagedObject, entityMapping mapping: NSEntityMapping,
        manager: NSMigrationManager) throws
    {
        try super.createDestinationInstancesForSourceInstance(sInstance,
            entityMapping: mapping, manager: manager)
        guard let continentCode = sInstance.isoContinent else { return }
        guard let country =
            manager.destinationInstancesForEntityMappingNamed(
                mapping.name, sourceInstances: [sInstance]).first
            else { fatalError("must return country") }
        guard let context = country.managedObjectContext
            else { fatalError("must have context") }
        let continent = context.findOrCreateContinent(continentCode)
        country.setContinent(continent)
    }
}
```

One peculiarity of the code in mapping policies is that you'll work a lot with
key-value coding on plain NSManagedObject instances, since you usually
don't have all the old versions of your model classes around anymore. To make
this safer and more readable, we define private extensions on
NSManagedObject that encapsulate those KVC calls right in the file of the
custom policy. By making these extensions private, they can't interfere with
the rest of our code. Please check the source code on GitHub[10] for the details.

In the code above, we first call the superclass's implementation, since we want
Core Data to migrate the country object as per the mapping model's
specification. Then we do the remaining migration through our custom logic:

1. We check if the source country has an isoContinent value and exit early if
   it doesn't.

2. We retrieve the newly created destination country object from the
   migration manager. Since this object has to be present (the call to super
   should have created it), we crash if it's not there. This code path should
   never happen.

3. We get the context of the destination object. Again, we indicate with a
   fatal error that the optional managedObjectContext property has to be
   non-nil at this point.

4. We find or create the continent object and set it on the country's continent to-one relationship.

The code in custom mapping policies is highly domain specific. In the example above, we split an existing entity into two. Another common case for a custom mapping policy is transforming existing attributes in non-trivial ways.

Migration and the UI

Migrations are potentially expensive operations, depending on the structure and the size of the dataset. You should profile your migrations on actual devices with real-world datasets to get a good estimate of how much time they really take. Usually, you have to make sure to offload this work to a background queue and present a sensible UI to the user, ideally with some progress reporting.

A common problem arises if the Core Data stack is set up in the application delegate and you then enable automatic migrations. The migration will run on the main queue, potentially blocking it for an extended period of time. During this time, the entire app will hang and the OS might even kill the app if the process takes too long.

One solution is to check the compatibility of the store with the current model version before trying to set up the stack and take different routes depending on the result:

```
public func createMoodyMainContext(progress: NSProgress? = nil,
    migrationCompletion: NSManagedObjectContext -> () = { _ in })
    -> NSManagedObjectContext?
{
    let version = MoodyModelVersion(storeURL: StoreURL)
    guard version == nil || version == MoodyModelVersion.CurrentVersion else {
        // the migration route ...
        return nil
    }
    let context = NSManagedObjectContext(
        concurrencyType: .MainQueueConcurrencyType,
        modelVersion: MoodyModelVersion.CurrentVersion, storeURL: StoreURL)
    return context
}
```

If we don't have an existing SQLite store yet, or if its version matches the current model version, we proceed as usual and return the context. However, if the version of the existing store is not equal to the current model version, we take the async migration route and exit early by returning nil.

In the calling code, we can now proceed to set up the normal UI if we immediately get back a managed object context. If we don't get back a context, we can show a migration UI and use the completion handler to show the main UI once the migration is done.

The actual migration code path simply dispatches onto a background queue and uses the same convenience initializer on NSManagedObjectContext to perform the migration and to instantiate the context once the migration is done. Then we dispatch back onto the main queue and call the migrationCompletion(_:) function:

```
dispatch_async(dispatch_get_global_queue(QOS_CLASS_USER_INITIATED, 0)) {
    let context = NSManagedObjectContext(
        concurrencyType: .MainQueueConcurrencyType,
        modelVersion: MoodyModelVersion.CurrentVersion, storeURL: StoreURL,
        progress: progress)
    dispatch_async(dispatch_get_main_queue()) {
        migrationCompletion(context)
    }
}
```

Some information about what's going on, together with a progress indicator, can go a long way in making the migration process less awkward for the user. The migration manager supports NSProgress, and we can leverage this in our custom migration function to report the progress of the overall migration process. For this, we first have to initialize a progress object with the number of migration steps as the total unit count. Then we make the progress object become the current progress each time we initialize a migration manager:

```
public func migrateStoreFromURL<Version: ModelVersionType>(
    sourceURL: NSURL, toURL: NSURL, targetVersion: Version,
    deleteSource: Bool = false, progress: NSProgress? = nil)
{
    // ...
    var migrationProgress: NSProgress?
    if let p = progress {
        migrationProgress = NSProgress(
            totalUnitCount: Int64(migrationSteps.count),
            parent: p, pendingUnitCount: p.totalUnitCount)
```

```
    }
    for step in migrationSteps {
        migrationProgress?.becomeCurrentWithPendingUnitCount(1)
        let manager = NSMigrationManager(sourceModel: step.sourceModel,
            destinationModel: step.destinationModel)
        migrationProgress?.resignCurrent()
        // ...
    }
    // ...
}
```

Testing Migrations

Migrating old data to be compatible with the current version of your app is a
crucial code path in your application. If you ship a bug in this part of your
code, chances are that after an update, your app will become unusable for
some or all users. You should go the extra mile and add automated tests for the
migrations from all potential source models to the target model.

In the migrations sample project, we use unit tests[11] to demonstrate how
migrations work, but you can also look at them as examples for how to test
your own migrations.

The basic principle is simple: for each potential migration path that can
happen in your app, you need an SQLite store with known data in the source
format, as well as a test fixture containing the expected data after the
migration to compare the result against.

The simplest way to obtain a valid SQLite store is to copy it from an
installation of the old application into the test target. You might want to prune
the store's content so that the test fixtures are reasonably small. Then you have
to extract the data (e.g. using the SQLite command line tool), change it in the
way it should change during the migration, and hardcode the expected result
in your testing code.

We create one struct per entity to hold the test data. Those structs all conform
to the following protocol:

```
protocol TestEntityDataType {
```

11https://github.com/objcio/core-data/blob/master/Migrations/MigrationsTests

```
    var entityName: String { get }
    func matchesManagedObject(mo: NSManagedObject) -> Bool
}
```

Implementing matchesManagedObject(_:) on each of these structs allows us to check whether or not the test data matches up with a managed object loaded from the migrated store. To make this comparison easier, we also create a TestVersionData struct that encapsulates the whole set of test fixture data for a certain model version. Then we add a method on TestVersionData that checks whether or not its data matches with the data in a given managed object context:

```
struct TestVersionData {
    let data: [[TestEntityDataType]]

    func matchWithContext(context: NSManagedObjectContext) -> Bool {
        for entityData in data {
            let request = NSFetchRequest(
                entityName: entityData.first!.entityName)
            let objects = try! context.executeFetchRequest(request)
                as! [NSManagedObject]
            guard objects.count == entityData.count else { return false }
            guard objects.all({ o in
                entityData.some { $0.matchesManagedObject(o) }
            }) else { return false }
        }
        return true
    }
}
```

We won't reproduce the code for the actual test fixtures here, since that's long, not very pretty, and not very interesting. However, you can find it all on GitHub[12].

Migration Debug Output

Core Data has a debug mode for migrations that you can enable by setting the launch argument:

-com.apple.CoreData.MigrationDebug 1

[12]https://github.com/objcio/core-data/blob/master/Migrations/MigrationsTests

This will output additional diagnostic information during the migration process, which can be helpful in debugging migration problems.

Summary

Once you have to change your data model, you must start using migrations to transform old data to match your current data model version. As always, Core Data offers a lot of flexibility in this process. You can let Core Data control the migration process, or you can control it yourself. You can let Core Data infer the mapping model between two model versions if the changes are simple enough, or you can create custom mapping models.

The bottom line is that you should choose the simplest approach that works for your use case and then add automated tests for all migrations that could happen in production.

Takeaways

→ Think about whether or not you have to migrate your data at all. Chances are that you might be able to just start fresh and re-download the data.

→ In a lot of cases, you can get away with using lightweight migrations.

→ If the changes to your model are more complicated, look into custom mapping models. For even more control, custom entity mapping policies are the way to go.

→ Core Data's automatic migration option requires you to maintain mapping models from all potential source model versions to the current version. If your data model changes rarely, that might still be the easiest option.

→ If you have to change your data model often, think about controlling the migration process yourself in order to enable progressive migrations.

→ Perform migration on a background queue and use progress reporting to give the user a sense of what's happening.

→ Always write automated tests for all potential migration paths that can happen in production. Migrations are typical examples of code paths that fall by the wayside in manual testing.

Profiling

13

We already talked about many aspects of ensuring great performance from Core Data in the dedicated chapter about performance. In this chapter, we'll focus on how to profile Core Data to determine exactly where performance bottlenecks occur and how you can use this information to improve your code.

The techniques demonstrated in this chapter are not only great for profiling your app; they can also help when you're trying to understand what's happening in the Core Data stack. For example, we used the first tool, Core Data's SQL debug output, a lot during the process of writing this book.

SQL Debug Output

The easiest way to gain insight into what Core Data is doing behind the scenes when you execute fetch requests, access properties, or save data is to use a launch argument to enable Core Data's SQL debug output:

-com.apple.CoreData.SQLDebug 1

You can set this argument in Xcode's scheme editor:

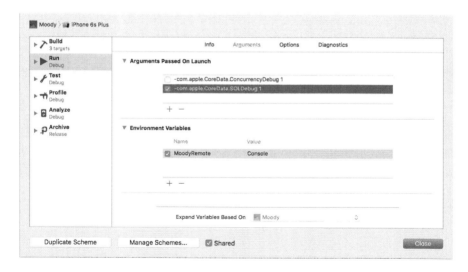

Figure 13.1: Specifying launch arguments in Xcode's scheme editor

To understand the output that's being printed to the console with this option, you should have a basic understanding of SQL. Please skip ahead to the appendix on relational databases and SQL if you're not yet familiar with it.

When we launch our sample app with the SQLDebug option enabled, the first line of output is something like this (we've removed the prefix to make it more succinct):

```
annotation: Connecting to sqlite database file at
    "/Users/florian/Library/Developer/CoreSimulator/Devices/
    4AE6C8E8-0F8F-4AE2-90DF-FD85E3289E75/data/Containers/Data/
    Application/9C2E68D8-E392-488E-9F92-B35FFC18A48E/Documents/
    Moody.moody"
```

Here, Core Data tells us which SQLite file it's using. This will come in handy later when we open this file directly with SQLite's command line utility.

Fetch Requests

When showing the regions table view controller, the following log output represents the fetch request backing the fetched results controller:

```
sql:  SELECT t0.Z_ENT, t0.Z_PK
    FROM ZGEOGRAPHICREGION t0
    WHERE t0.ZMARKEDFORDELETIONDATE = ?
    ORDER BY t0.ZUPDATEDAT DESC
annotation: sql connection fetch time: 0.0004s
annotation: total fetch execution time: 0.0007s for 5 rows.
```

The first line is the SQL statement executed by SQLite, where we can see that the ZGEOGRAPHICREGION table, which corresponds to the *GeographicRegion* entity we defined in the data model, is accessed. From this table, the columns Z_ENT and Z_PK are retrieved, the former being the identifier of the entity and the latter being the row's primary key. The search in this table is constrained by the WHERE clause to rows that are not marked for deletion. We also see the sort descriptor applied to the query using the ORDER BY clause on the updatedAt attribute.

From a profiling point of view, the next two lines are interesting: Core Data first tells us the time this query took SQLite to execute (0.4 ms in this case). It then reports the total time for this request, which includes the extra work Core

Data has to do on top of the SQLite query (0.7 ms in this case). We also learn about the number of rows the query returned.

Because we configured this fetch request with a fetchBatchSize, the query shown above does not retrieve any of the actual data — it only fetches the objects' primary keys to construct the batched results array. The next output statements show the query made to fetch the actual data for the first batch:

```
sql:  SELECT t0.Z_ENT, t0.Z_PK, t0.Z_OPT, t0.ZMARKEDFORDELETIONDATE,
         t0.ZNUMBEROFMOODS, t0.ZNUMERICISO3166CODE,
         t0.ZUNIQUENESSDUMMY, t0.ZUPDATEDAT, t0.ZNUMBEROFCOUNTRIES,
         t0.ZCONTINENT
      FROM ZGEOGRAPHICREGION t0
      WHERE t0.Z_PK IN (SELECT * FROM _Z_intarray0)
      LIMIT 20
annotation: sql connection fetch time: 0.0018s
annotation: total fetch execution time: 0.0034s for 6 rows.
```

Structurally, this output is the same as the one above, but the query is a bit more complicated. We see all columns being requested from the geographic region table with a fetch limit of 20: our fetchBatchSize. We also see only a subset of rows being requested using the WHERE clause. Core Data uses a subquery to constrain the query, but the details of this are not important for our purposes here.

This kind of output is already extremely helpful when profiling performance issues. We learn about the exact time each fetch request took and can narrow down where the problem lies.

We can also use this output to dive deeper and analyze the queries Core Data sends to SQLite. To do that, we use SQLite's command line utility to open the database file directly. On the SQLite prompt, we can use the "EXPLAIN QUERY PLAN"[1] command to learn how SQLite processes an SQL statement.

For example, we can analyze the first query from above like this:

```
$ sqlite3 <moody-document-dir>/Moody.moody
sqlite> EXPLAIN QUERY PLAN
      SELECT t0.Z_ENT, t0.Z_PK FROM ZGEOGRAPHICREGION t0
      WHERE t0.ZMARKEDFORDELETIONDATE = ?
      ORDER BY t0.ZUPDATEDAT DESC;
```

---

1 https://www.sqlite.org/eqp.html

This will result in the following output:

```
0|0|0|SEARCH TABLE ZGEOGRAPHICREGION AS t0
    USING INDEX ZGEOGRAPHICREGION_ZMARKEDFORDELETIONDATE_INDEX
    (ZMARKEDFORDELETIONDATE=?)
0|0|0|USE TEMP B-TREE FOR ORDER BY
```

> You can instruct SQLite to format the output in a more verbose, but
> easier to read way by entering the following two commands on the
> SQLite prompt: .mode columns and .header on.

The first line indicates that SQLite performs a search (SEARCH TABLE) in the
ZGEOGRAPHICREGION table using the index on markedForDeletionDate to
order the rows. The second line tells us that SQLite then constructs a
temporary index on the fly for the ORDER BY clause, which sorts the results in
descending order, according to the updatedAt attribute. If we try to improve
upon this situation by adding an index on updatedAt, the result might be
surprising:

```
0|0|0|SEARCH TABLE ZGEOGRAPHICREGION AS t0
    USING INDEX ZGEOGRAPHICREGION_ZMARKEDFORDELETIONDATE_INDEX
        (ZMARKEDFORDELETIONDATE=?)
0|0|0|USE TEMP B-TREE FOR ORDER BY
```

Wait a second — that's the same as before! Although we now have an index on
the updatedAt attribute, SQLite is still not using it for sorting. That's because
SQLite uses a maximum of one index per table, and it already used the index
on markedForDeletionDate to filter the rows. However, we can create a
compound index that includes both markedForDeletionDate and updatedAt, in
this order:

Figure 13.2: Creating a compound index in the Data Model Inspector

Running EXPLAIN QUERY PLAN again now shows the compound index on both markedForDeletionDate and updatedAt being used:

```
0|0|0|SEARCH TABLE ZGEOGRAPHICREGION AS t0
    USING INDEX
    ZGEOGRAPHICREGION_ZMARKEDFORDELETIONDATE_ZUPDATEDAT
    (ZMARKEDFORDELETIONDATE=?)
```

With this compound index in place, we can remove the single index on markedForDeletionDate, since SQLite can use compound indexes partially. For example, a compound index over three attributes can be used for a predicate that only filters by the first attribute, by the first two, or by all of the attributes in the compound index. However, the compound index cannot be used for a predicate that only filters by the compound index's second or third attribute.

We take advantage of a compound index on the *Mood* entity as well. The fetch request we use to display moods in a table view has a predicate (filtering the moods where both markedForDeletionDate and markedForRemoteDeletion are **false**) and a sort descriptor (on date). In the SQL debug output, the request looks like this:

```
sql: SELECT 0, t0.Z_PK FROM ZMOOD t0
    WHERE (( t0.ZMARKEDFORDELETIONDATE = ?
            AND t0.ZMARKEDFORREMOTEDELETION = ?
            ) AND t0.ZCOUNTRY = ?)
    ORDER BY t0.ZDATE DESC
annotation: sql connection fetch time: 0.0006s
```

annotation: total fetch execution time: 0.0009s **for** 44 rows.

With a compound index on markedForRemoteDeletion,
markedForDeletionDate, and date, the output of EXPLAIN QUERY PLAN for the
statement looks like this:

```
0|0|0|SEARCH TABLE ZMOOD AS t0
    USING INDEX
    ZMOOD_ZMARKEDFORREMOTEDELETION_ZMARKEDFORDELETIONDATE_ZDATE
    (ZMARKEDFORREMOTEDELETION=? AND ZMARKEDFORDELETIONDATE=?)
```

The compound index can serve the predicate as well as the sort order. Note
that SQLite has optimized the order of the predicates to be able to use the
compound index; markedForDeletionDate was the first condition in our
original predicate, whereas SQLite puts it in second place, since it is in second
place in the compound index as well.

The advantage of ordering the attributes in the compound index this way is
that the same index can now also be used by the syncing engine to query for
moods that have their markedForRemoteDeletion attribute set to **true.**

SQLite's documentation of its query planner[2] is a very good resource for
learning more about how indexes are used and how you can optimize them to
get the best performance for your particular queries.

Using EXPLAIN QUERY PLAN is an extremely powerful tool to analyze what
SQLite is doing under the hood. As we saw above, you can find out if and how
indexes are being used. Together with the profiling information from Core
Data's debug output, you no longer have to guess if changes you make to your
data model or to your fetch requests improve performance or not, because you
have detailed information and performance measurements to base your
decisions on.

Fulfilling Faults

Core Data's SQL debug output also indicates whenever a fault is fulfilled from
the database. For example, if we'd set includesPropertyValues to **false** on the
fetch request for the regions table view, we'd see additional output like this in
the console:

---

2 https://www.sqlite.org/queryplanner.html

```
sql:  SELECT t0.Z_ENT, t0.Z_PK, t0.Z_OPT, t0.ZMARKEDFORDELETIONDATE,
         t0.ZNUMBEROFMOODS, t0.ZNUMERICISO3166CODE,
         t0.ZUNIQUENESSDUMMY, t0.ZUPDATEDAT, t0.ZNUMBEROFCOUNTRIES,
         t0.ZCONTINENT
      FROM ZGEOGRAPHICREGION t0
      WHERE  t0.Z_PK = ?
annotation: sql connection fetch time: 0.0005s
annotation: total fetch execution time: 0.0008s for 1 rows.
annotation: fault  fulfilled  from database for : 0xd000000000100002
      <x-coredata://DE6497F9-8B94-420D-81B7-E25B992E28C2/Country/p4>
```

The output is similar to what we saw for fetch requests above, but you can already see in the query's WHERE clause that Core Data is only asking for one row with a particular primary key. The last line explicitly tells you that this query was used to fulfill a fault for a certain object ID.

When you see many of those "fault fulfilled from database" statements in the console in a short time, this tells you that Core Data has to make many round trips to the database to fetch the data your app needs, one object at a time, which is very inefficient. The reason for this is usually a badly configured fetch request, as in our example above.

Saving Data

When we save a new mood, the following debug output appears in the console:

```
sql: BEGIN EXCLUSIVE
sql: SELECT Z_MAX FROM Z_PRIMARYKEY WHERE Z_ENT = ?
sql: UPDATE Z_PRIMARYKEY SET Z_MAX = ? WHERE Z_ENT = ? AND Z_MAX = ?
sql: COMMIT
sql: BEGIN EXCLUSIVE
sql: INSERT INTO
     ZMOOD(Z_PK, Z_ENT, Z_OPT, ZCOUNTRY, ZCOLORS, ZDATE, ZLATITUDE,
        ZLONGITUDE, ZMARKEDFORDELETIONDATE,
        ZMARKEDFORREMOTEDELETION, ZREMOTEIDENTIFIER)
     VALUES(?, ?, ?, ?, ?, ?, ?, ?, ?, ?, ?)
sql: UPDATE ZGEOGRAPHICREGION SET ZUPDATEDAT = ?, Z_OPT = ?
     WHERE Z_PK = ? AND Z_OPT = ?
sql: COMMIT
```

The above lines tell us exactly what's happening during the save. First, Core Data gets the current maximum primary key from the Z_PRIMARYKEY table and increases it with a subsequent UPDATE statement. Those two SQL statements are wrapped in a transaction (BEGIN EXCLUSIVE and COMMIT) to make sure nobody else is writing to the database at the same time. Then the new mood gets inserted, and the updatedAt attribute on the corresponding region is updated. Again, those two statements are wrapped in a transaction.

Contrary to fetch requests, the SQL debug output doesn't tell us how long a save request took to execute. However, we can get this information using the Core Data instruments, as we'll describe next.

Core Data Instruments

Instruments comes with a couple of special Core Data instruments that you can use to profile your app's persistency performance. You can combine any of these Core Data instruments with other instruments — such as the Time Profiler, Allocations, or I/O Activity — to record a comprehensive profile of your app.

The predefined Core Data template includes the Fetches, Saves, and Cache Misses instruments. However, there's one more you can select from the Instruments library: the Faults instrument.

In the screenshot below, we use a custom template with all four Core Data instruments, along with the Time Profiler instrument next to them:

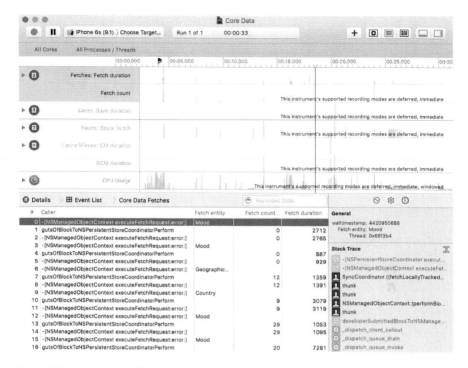

Figure 13.3: Instruments with the Fetches, Saves, Faults, and Cache Misses instruments

The Core Data instruments provide you with the following metrics:

1. Fetches

   You can see exactly how often fetch requests happen, how many objects they return, and how long they take.

2. Saves

   Similar to fetch requests, the Saves instrument shows how often saves happen and how much time each save takes.

3. Faults

   The Faults instrument shows you the object and relationship faults that Core Data has to fulfill. In the detail view, you can see the object IDs and the relationship names of the faults being fulfilled, as well as the durations of these operations.

4. Cache Misses

In the cache misses track, you can see how many of the faults being triggered had to be fulfilled from SQLite because the data was not yet present in the store's row cache. As with the Faults instrument, cache misses are reported separately for object and relationship faults. In the detail view, you can see which objects caused those cache misses and how long the round trip to SQLite took.

For all the events recorded by the Core Data instruments, you can inspect the call stack in the extended detail view. This tells you from which part of your code the selected event originated.

The graphical presentation of all the Core Data-related metrics can give you a very good idea how all the parts play together and where bottlenecks occur.

For example, take a look at the following trace of the Fetches, Faults, and Cache Misses instruments:

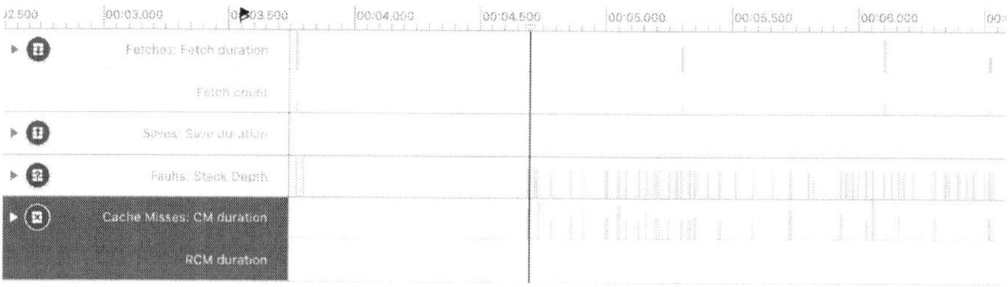

Figure 13.4: The Faults and Cache Misses instruments show faults that were fulfilled from the SQLite store

This trace was recorded after starting up the *Moody* sample app. The first fetch request in the trace is the initial fetch backing the fetched results controller of the moods table view. Then we start scrolling down the table view, triggering some more fetch requests as new batches of data get pulled in.

The interesting part, though, is that of the other two tracks: faults and cache misses. Here you can see a lot of faults being fulfilled. Looking at the detail view tells us that those faults are Country objects:

Figure 13.5: The detail view of the Cache Misses instrument shows which objects caused the round trips to SQLite

Core Data had to retrieve the data for lots of those faults from SQLite. This is indicated by the lines in the cache misses track that match up to the lines in the faults track above. Going back to SQLite that often could cause a noticeable stutter during scrolling.

This happens because we show the name of each mood's country: to configure a mood table view cell, we have to access the country relationship on the Mood object to get the ISO code of the corresponding country.

One way to tackle this issue would be to denormalize our data model, i.e. we could store the country code directly in the *Mood* entity. However, in this case, we'll take a different route and prefetch the country objects for the moods table view. When we want to show all moods, we simply prefetch all countries (we can do that because we know that the maximum number of countries is pretty small):

```
extension MoodSource {
    func prefetchInContext(context: NSManagedObjectContext)
        -> [MoodyModel.Country]
    {
        switch self {
        case .All: ()
            return MoodyModel.Country.fetchInContext(context) { request in
                request.predicate = MoodyModel.Country.defaultPredicate
            }
        // ...
        }
    }
}
```

With this prefetching in place, the trace now looks like this:

Figure 13.6: After prefetching the needed Country objects fulfilling the faults no longer causes cache misses

As you can see, all the lines in the cache misses track are now gone. There are still a lot of Country object faults being fulfilled, but the data for those objects has already been loaded into the row cache. We could go one step further and require the country objects to be prefetched as materialized objects. This would make the lines in the faults trace disappear, but there's no need for that in our example.

Threading Guard

Similar to the SQL debug launch argument, there's another argument you can specify (as of iOS 8 and OS X 10.10):

-com.apple.CoreData.ConcurrencyDebug 1

Running your app with this argument helps to debug threading issues: Core Data will throw an exception whenever you access a managed object or managed object context from the wrong queue.

Summary

Before you attempt to optimize your Core Data code, it's important to diagnose the performance bottlenecks first. Using the SQL debug launch argument and the Core Data instruments, you can get precise profiling metrics and gain deep insights into what Core Data is doing behind the scenes.

If you work with multiple contexts on different queues, the concurrency debug launch argument can save you a lot of debugging work if you run into threading issues.

Relational Database Basics and SQL

14

The default store of Core Data is the SQLite store. Most of the concepts of Core Data are designed around how the SQLite store works, and in this chapter we will take a closer look at them. You don't need to know everything we discuss here in order to use Core Data, but it's very helpful when trying to understand its inner workings.

A word of warning: this chapter will skip some details, and it presents relational databases in the way they're used by Core Data. As such, the focus is on understanding the aforementioned things. In particular, we won't go into details about creating tables and inserting data. These may seem like basics but are not at all important for our purpose.

An Embedded Database

The SQLite store is built around a relational database. It runs inside your app — there is no separate database process that your app connects to. Core Data *talks* in the *structured query language* (SQL) to the database API. Whenever Core Data wants the database to do something (e.g. retrieve data or modify data), Core Data will generate a so-called SQL statement, such as the following:

SELECT 0, t0.Z_PK FROM ZPERSON t0

It will then send this string to the SQLite API. Core Data is using SQLite, which is a particular implementation of a relational database on iOS and OS X.

SQLite parses the SQL statements that Core Data sends to it and executes them. In turn, the SQLite library reads or writes to the database in the file system. Some SQL databases run independently of the application using them. SQLite, however, is embedded: it is part of the app, and there's no separate process for it:

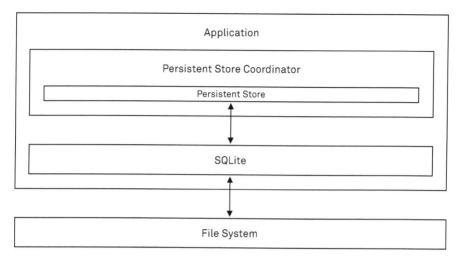

Figure 14.1: The components of the persistence layer

The model for relational databases was first formulated around 1970. Although the world of computing has changed dramatically since then, relational databases are still solid workhorses for persisting both small and large amounts of structured data.

Tables, Columns, and Rows

The data inside a relational database is organized into tables. A table may look something like this:

key	name	favorite food
1	Miguel	Bruschetta
2	Melissa	Bagel
3	Ben	Bacon

A table is also referred to as a *relation*, hence the name relational database: a database based on tables.

Data inside a table is subsequently organized into columns. In this example, key, name, and favorite food are the columns. The three rows are entries in this table.

Relational databases have a so-called *schema*. It describes which tables the database has and which *attributes* or columns each table has. Data can only be stored according to the defined schema.

When using SQL, it is quite common to add a so-called *primary key* attribute to a table, and Core Data does just that. This attribute — usually an integer — uniquely identifies each row. When a new row is inserted, the database automatically assigns a new (incremented) value to the new row's primary key.

Architecture of the Database System

A typical database system can be split into four components: a *query processor* that takes the statements in the SQL language and processes them; a *storage manager* that manages buffers in memory and storage inside files in the file system; a *transaction manager* that ensures the integrity of the database; and finally, the *data and metadata* stored in the file system:

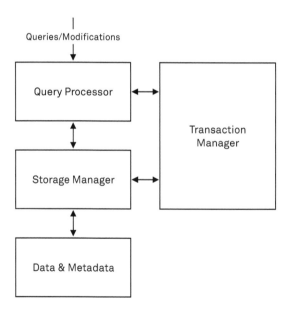

Figure 14.2: The components of a typical relational database system

The implementation of SQLite is structured into slightly different blocks[1], but the concepts remain unchanged.

Query Processor

Below, we will take a quick look at how the SQL language can be used. When someone sends SQL statements to the database, the *query processor* takes these and turns them into a sequence of requests and actions to be performed on the stored data.

An important task of the query processor is to optimize queries: it creates a so-called *query plan*, which describes the optimal way to retrieve data. Based on the SQL statement and the existence of indexes, the query processor will decide whether or not it is beneficial to consult indexes.

Storage Manager

The storage manager takes care of the storage of data in the file system, the memory used by the page cache, and the interactions between the two.

The way SQLite uses the file system is quite complex and far beyond the scope of this chapter. The storage manager's role is to take care of how data is stored and retrieved. Dramatically simplifying things, we can assume that data is stored in a file that, in turn, consists of equally large so-called pages. SQLite will keep some of these pages in memory. This is the SQLite page cache.

Transaction Manager

SQLite is a transactional database. Transactions ensure that all changes within a single transaction are either committed wholly or not at all. SQLite does this by relying on a set of properties known as ACID, which ensures that all changes and queries appear to be Atomic, Consistent, Isolated, and Durable.

Core Data uses transactions to ensure that a call to the context's save(_:) method is transactional as well.

1 https://www.sqlite.org/arch.html

As mentioned above, a transaction is guaranteed to be committed to the database in its entirety or not at all. If it fails due to an error — or even a crash or power loss — the database remains the same, as if the transaction had never happened.

This is a very important aspect of an SQLite store: even when the application crashes, or there's a kernel panic or a power failure, the database will remain in a consistent state. None of these kinds of events will ever corrupt it.

In fact, the only way to corrupt an SQLite-based Core Data store is to interact with the database files directly. That's why you should always use the Core Data API to move or copy a database.

Data and Metadata

The last building block of the database is the data and metadata of the database, i.e. the things that are stored. The actual data, the content of the database, and the metadata such as the database schema and indexes are all persisted in the file system.

The schema defines which tables the database has — along with their names — and for each table, it also defines the attributes of that table and the attributes' names. This data is stored inside the database files.

We'll briefly mention indexes below. They can improve the speed of querying the database, and the index data is persisted inside the database files too.

The Database Language SQL

Let's say we have the following table, named *Movie*, in our database:

id	title	year
1	City of God	2002
2	12 Angry Men	1957
3	The Shawshank Redemption	1994

We can perform simple queries on the database like this:

```
SELECT id, title, year FROM Movie WHERE year = 1994;
```

This returns the tuple for *The Shawshank Redemption*:

```
3 | The Shawshank Redemption | 1994
```

Most simple SQL queries are built using the three keywords SELECT, FROM, and WHERE. The query specifies which attributes to retrieve (id, title, and year), from which table (Movie), and which conditions to match. If we wanted to know which movies are from before the year 2000, we could execute the following:

```
SELECT id FROM Movie WHERE year < 2000;
```

We'd then get this as the result:

```
2
3
```

Alternately, we could ask for all attributes:

```
SELECT id, title, year FROM Movie WHERE year < 2000;
```

This would produce the following:

```
2 | 12 Angry Men            | 1957
3 | The Shawshank Redemption | 1994
```

Or, given a specific *id*, we could retrieve the corresponding row:

```
SELECT id, title, year FROM Movie WHERE id = 3;
```

In doing so, we'd get this:

```
3 | The Shawshank Redemption | 1994
```

The *id* attribute in this sample is the *primary key*, and it corresponds to what Core Data uses to create the object identifier. Retrieving a single element by its id corresponds to Core Data fulfilling a fault from SQLite. The id is equivalent to the object identifier in Core Data. Getting just the *id* values corresponds to what Core Data does when using fetch batch size.

Sorting

We can let the database sort the results using ORDER BY:

```
SELECT id, title, year FROM Movie WHERE year > 1990 ORDER BY year;
```

In doing so, we'd get the following:

```
3 | The Shawshank Redemption | 1994
1 | City of God              | 2002
```

This also works when we sort on *year* but only retrieve the *id* attribute:

```
SELECT id FROM Movie WHERE year > 1990 ORDER BY year;
```

```
3
1
```

For large datasets, we can add an index on a table for a given attribute. This makes it extremely efficient for the database to sort or search on that attribute.

When setting sort descriptors on a fetch request, Core Data will add a corresponding ORDER BY clause to the SELECT statement it generates. This way, the database does the heavy lifting, which is way more efficient than sorting data once it's been retrieved from the database. When using a fetch request with the *fetch batch size* set, Core Data can also retrieve a list of just the object identifiers and still have them be sorted according to the sort descriptors.

Relationships

There are many ways to implement relationships. We will look at the three cases — one-to-one, one-to-many, and many-to-many — and see conceptually how Core Data handles each of these.

One-To-One

We can create a one-to-one relationship based on the *id* field, i.e. what would correspond to the *object identifier* in Core Data.

Say we have an *Image* table for images:

id	url	width	height
1	http://www.imdb.com/images/12.jpg	67	98

If we want to create a one-to-one relationship so that each movie has a *title image*, we will add a column or attribute to both the *Image* and the *Movie* tables. We will call these *titleImage* and *titleImageOf*, respectively:

id	title	year	titleImage
2	12 Angry Men	1957	1

id	url	width	height	titleImageOf
1	http://www.imdb.com/images/12.jpg	67	98	2

We now have to make sure that whenever we update or delete an entry in either of the *Image* or the *Movie* tables, the other side gets updated too. For instance, if we delete the row with *id* 1 in the *Image* table, we'd have to remove the *titleImage* attribute of the corresponding *Movie* row.

This is how Core Data implements one-to-one relationships.

One-To-Many

One-to-many relationships work slightly differently. If we want to relate multiple *Image* rows to a single *Movie*, it is infeasible to add backreferences from a particular *Movie* row to all related *Image* rows.

Instead, we can add a *movie* attribute to each *Image* row:

id	url	width	height	movie
1	http://www.imdb.com/images/12-a.jpg	67	98	2
2	http://www.imdb.com/images/12-b.jpg	67	94	2
3	http://www.imdb.com/images/12-c.jpg	67	94	2
4	http://www.imdb.com/images/CoG-a.jpg	72	102	1

It's trivial to look up the movie of a given image. But we can easily find the *id* of all related *Image* rows for a given *Movie* row with the following:

```
SELECT id FROM Image WHERE movie == 2;
```

Using the above, we'd get this:

```
1
2
3
```

This is how Core Data implements one-to-many relationships.

Many-To-Many

Finally, many-to-many relationships cannot feasibly be implemented by adding attributes to either of the existing tables. As such, we need to create another table.

Consider this table of people, called *Person*:

id	name
1	Sidney Lumet
2	Kátia Lund
3	Frank Darabont
4	Fernando Meirelles

What we want is a many-to-many relationship between *Movie* and *Person* for the directors of movies. A movie can have multiple directors, and a director can have multiple movies.

We can do this by adding another table, *Director*, with these entries:

movie	director
1	2
1	4
2	1
3	3

With this, we can get the directors of *City of God*:

```
SELECT p.id, p.name FROM Person p JOIN Director d ON p.id == d.director
WHERE d.movie = 1;
```

We're using the JOIN keyword to join the *Director* table with the *Person* table based on the *Person* table's *id* and the *Director* table's *director* attribute. Then, from within that joined result, we SELECT the results where the *movie* attribute of the *Director* table is *1*, corresponding to *City of God*.

This is how Core Data implements many-to-many relationships.

Transactions

As mentioned above, SQLite implements a transactional database engine, meaning all statements in a transaction will either fail or succeed as a whole. Core Data uses this to make calls to save(_:) transactional. It does so by putting a BEGIN EXCLUSIVE before the statements that change the database and a COMMIT after these statements. That way, they're grouped into a transaction.

Any changes to be made are inserted between these two. Since it's an exclusive transaction, a lock has to be acquired. No other connection is able to write to the database after the BEGIN EXCLUSIVE until the COMMIT has been processed.

Indexes

In order to search for specific rows, or to sort the returned result by a specific attribute, SQLite has to look at all rows in the database, unless it has an index for the given attribute.

An index improves the performance of retrieving data from the database. This improvement comes at the cost of a larger database file size, and it makes changes to the database (inserts, updates, deletes) more expensive, since these have to update the indexes.

SQLite allows an index to be created on a single attribute or a combination of attributes.

Consider the following example:

```
CREATE INDEX MovieYear ON Movie (year);
```

Here, the database creates an index for the *year* attribute of the *Movie* table, and any future changes to the *Movie* table will automatically cause the index to be updated.

We go into much more detail about how to determine if you should add indexes to your database — and if so, which ones — in the chapter about profiling. SQLite can print out which query plan the query processor is generating for a given SELECT statement. This query plan shows if indexes are being used, and if so, which ones.

Journaling

By default, the SQLite database that Core Data creates uses Write-Ahead Logging (WAL)[2] to journal the file. This makes corruption impossible: your database cannot be corrupted unless you use any API other than Core Data (or SQLite) to operate on the database files.

WAL journaling is implemented so that reading and writing can proceed concurrently: readers do not block writers, and a writer does not block readers. With Core Data, this is relevant when using multiple persistent store coordinators (as we've shown in the concurrency chapter), or even when using multiple processes to access the same database.

When using a database with WAL, there are two additional files in the file system: a "-wal" file and an "-shm" file. These are used to implement the journaling.

Something to be aware of is that with WAL, large commits (with more than 100 MB of data) will be comparatively slow. When using Core Data, this is less likely to be an issue, since large commits correspond to a large Core Data changeset being saved. This is something you should generally avoid, since it also incurs a larger memory footprint, regardless of WAL.

It is possible to change SQLite to use a different journaling method. We talk more about that in the performance chapter.

---

2 https://www.sqlite.org/draft/wal.html

Summary

This chapter shows how data inside an SQLite database is organized into multiple tables. Each table is very simple. Relationships between tables have to be built by referring to the *primary key* of another table. We talked about how the database is structured around four main parts: the *query processor*, the *transaction manager*, the *storage manager*, and the actual *data and metadata*. Finally, we mentioned that SQLite ensures ACID properties: the database is transactional and cannot be corrupted by errors or crashes.

Printed in Great Britain
by Amazon